Traveler's Guide to Greek

A quick start guide for conversing in Greek

Stavros Pappas

Table of Contents

For Emily

Introduction

Welcome to the quick start Traveler's Guide guide to learning spoken Greek. This pronunciation guide uses transliteration to help you learn spoken Greek quickly without having to master Greek script. The word transliteration means to write Greek words in the English alphabet such as to represent the sound of the Greek words. Each word is marked to show which syllable must stressed when you pronounce it.

This will let you rapidly learn Greek words so that you can understand and converse in Greek. This guide is ideal for travelers to Greece who would like to find their own way about Greece and to understand and speak to Greeks that they meet. Whether you are travelling to Greece for business or pleasure this guide will enhance your experience.

This guide will teach you some grammar as well as vocabulary that will be very useful in various situations like shopping, visiting a restaurant, exploring Athens, or renting a car. It will also cover typical phrases that you will find useful in conversations that you will have with native Greeks. It also includes the Greek alphabet as well as a mini English-Greek and Greek-English dictionaries and a set of verb tables.

The guide is phonetic, so you will pronounce each letter that you see in the transliterated words. All transliterated Greek words are shown in **bold** type. All letters of the transliteration alphabet will be lower case. All words are also shown in their Greek form to help you become accustomed to the Greek script and as an aid when conversing with Greek people.

Sections on grammar will be marked with G.

Let us start with some easy Greek words to introduce you to Greek. **ya su** means 'hello'.

The word **kali<u>mer</u>a** means 'Good day'. Notice the underlined <u>mer</u> in **kali<u>mer</u>a**, this means that the syllable is stressed like 'ka-li-<u>mer</u>-a'. All stressed syllables in this book will be shown underlined. Written Greek words also have an accent mark over the letter of the syllable that is stressed. For example **καλημέρα.**

1

Soon you will be able to recognize the stressed syllables. When starting to pronounce Greek words really emphasize the stressed syllable so you can get accustomed to its sound. Which syllable is stressed is important because changing the stress can alter the meaning of a word.

This guide will not provide perfect pronunciation but will be sufficient to help travelers make themselves understood in most cases.

Greek Alphabet

The Greek alphabet has 24 letters. The letters are listed below with their pronunciation guide word, the uppercase and lower case Greek letter, and also the sound that they make.

alfa	άλφα	Α α	'a' as in 'bag'
vita	βήτα	Β β	'v' as in 'vice'
gama	γάμμα	Γ γ	'y' as in 'yell' before 'e' and 'i', otherwise 'g' as in 'gun'
thelta	δέλτα	Δ δ	'th' as in 'they'
epsilon	έψιλον	Ε ε	'e' as in 'red'
zita	ζήτα	Ζ ζ	'z' as in 'zoo'
ita	ήτα	Η η	'i' as in 'ill'
thita	θήτα	Θ θ	'th' as in 'thin'
yota	ιώτα	Ι ι	'i' as in 'ill'
kappa	κάππα	Κ κ	'k' as in 'kite'
lamtha	λάμδα	Λ λ	'l' as in 'lion'
mi	μι	Μ μ	'm' as in 'mite'
ni	νι	Ν ν	'n' as in 'no'
ksi	ξι	Ξ ξ	'ks' as in 'weeks' or 'x' as in 'extra'
omicron	όμικρον	Ο ο	'o' as in 'cot'

2

pi	πι	Π π	'p' as in 'pea'
ro	ρο	Ρ ρ	rolled 'r' as in 'red'
sigma	σίγμα	Σ σ ς	's' as in 'sod'
taf	ταυ	Τ τ	't' as in 'toe'
ipsilon	ύπσιλον	Υ υ	'i' as in 'ill'
fi	φι	Φ φ	'f' as in 'fat'
chi	χι	Χ χ	'h' as in 'Hugh'
psi	ψι	Ψ ψ	'ps' as in 'lips'
omega	ωμέγα	Ω ω	'o' as in 'cot'

The following vowels are pronounced the same:

η, ι, υ (ita, yota, ipsilon): 'i' as in 'ill'

ο, ω (omikron, omega): 'o' as in 'cot'

Greek is written from left to right.

Letter Pairs

Greek has letter pairs that together form a single sound:

αι	'e' as in 'red'
ει, οι, υι	'i' as in 'ill'
ου	'u' as in 'put'
αυ	'av' as in 'average'
ευ	'ev' as in 'ever'
γκ	'g' as in 'get' at beginning of a word, 'ng' within a word
μπ	'b' as in 'bag' at beginning of a word, 'mb' within a word
ντ	'd' as in 'dog' at beginning of a word, 'nd' within a word
γγ	'ng' as in 'angle'

Here are some examples:

and	ke	και
yes	ne	ναι
my	mu	μου
He/she/it is	ine	είναι
bar	bar	μπαρ
shower	duz	ντους

Vowels (G)

You will notice that most Greek words end with a vowel. Let's go over how the Greek vowels sound. In this guide there is only one sound for each vowel to make the transliteration alphabet as simple as possible. This makes the pronunciation of Greek words straightforward.   There are only five vowel sounds which represent these Greek letters and letter pairs.

Vowel	Sound	Greek letters
a	'a' as in 'bag'	α
e	'e' as in 'red'	ε, αι
i	'i' as in 'ill'	η, ι, υ, ει, οι, υι
o	'o' as in 'cot'	ο, ω
u	'u' as in 'put'	ου

The words below are shown with their separate syllables to demonstrate their pronounication.

A α

The vowel 'a' is pronounced like 'a' sound in 'bag' or 'cat'. Here are some Greek words with the 'a' vowel:

Please.	pa-ra-ka-<u>lo</u>	Παρακαλώ

good	ka-<u>los</u>	καλός
Good day	ka-li-<u>mer</u>-a	Καλημέρα.

Again, notice the stressed syllable.

E ε, αι

The vowel 'e' is pronounced like 'e' in 'egg' or 'red'. Here are some Greek words with 'e':

I	e-<u>go</u>	εγώ
I am staying	<u>me</u>-no	μένω
warm	zes-<u>tos</u>	ζεστός
yes	ne	ναι
and	ke	και
He/she/it is	<u>ine</u>	είναι

Ι η, ι, υ, ει, οι, υι

In this guide the 'i' is pronounced like the 'i' in 'ill'. It also sounds like the 'e' in the words 'be' or 'we'. Here are some Greek words with the 'i' vowel:

how	ti	τι
city	<u>po</u>-lis	πόλης
Good day	ka-li-<u>mer</u>-a	καλημέρα.
Greek	e-li-ni-<u>ka</u>	ελληνικά
very	po-<u>li</u>	πολύ
there	e-<u>ki</u>	εκεί

O o, ω

Pronounce '**o**' as in 'cot' or 'log'. Here are some Greek words with the 'o' vowel:

how	pos	πώσ
the	to	το
new	ne-os	νέος
from	a-po	από
goodbye	a-thi-o	αντίο

U ου

Pronounce '**u**' as in 'cure' or 'pure'. It also sounds like the 'oo' in the words 'boot' or 'ooze'. Here are some Greek words with the 'u' vowel:

my	mu	μου
where	pu	πού
museum	mu-si-o	μουσείο
We want	the-lu-me	Θέλουμε

Practise saying these words slowly so you get familiar with their sound. Say each new word you learn aloud. That's it for pronouncing Greek vowels. Let's move on!

Consonants (G)

Most Greek consonants are pronounced the same as in English, however, there are a couple that need some explanation.

gama γ

The letter **gama** is pronounced in two different ways:

Before the vowels 'a', 'o' and 'u' and other consonants as a soft 'g". In this guide this is represented as 'g'. Here are some examples:

the letter gamma	ga-ma	γάμμα
late	ar-ga	αργά
milk	ga-la	γάλα
a little, some	li-go	λίγο
I	e-go	εγώ
knee	go-na-to	γόνατο
song	tra-gu-di	τραγούδι
I write (v)	gra-fo	γράφω

Before 'e' and 'i' as '**y**' as in 'yell'. In this guide this is represented as '**y**'. Here are some examples:

doctor	ya-tros	γιατρός
why	ya-ti	γιατί
wife	yi-ne-ka	γυναικά
son	yi-os	γιός
bye	ya	γεια
grandmother	ya-ya	γιαγιά
swimsuit	ma-yi-o	μαγιώ
full	ye-ma-tos	γεμάτος
meal	yev-ma	γεύμα
I go (v)	pi-ye-no	πηγαίνω

chi χ

Chi is pronounced with a throaty breathed sound as the 'h' in the name 'hugh'. In this guide this is represented as '**h**'. Here are some words with the chi sound:

the letter Chi	hi	χή
Hello.	<u>he</u>-re-te	χαίρετε.
Thank you.	ef-ha-ri-s<u>to</u>	ευχαριστώ.
juice	hi-<u>mos</u>	χυπός
time	<u>hro</u>-nos	χρόνος

Pronunciation

When learning to say a Greek word it is useful to split the word into its syllables and then first say the last syllable. Next say the preceding syllable and the last syllable together. Repeat this until you have pronounced the whole word. For example, the word parak<u>alo</u> (please). Split into syllables: pa-ra-ka-<u>lo</u>. Say -lo, then ka-<u>lo</u>, then ra-ka-<u>lo</u>, then pa-ra-ka-<u>lo</u>. Remember to stress the underlined syllable.

Eliding

Sometimes a vowel may be dropped when a word ends with a vowel and is followed by a word that starts with a vowel. One of the vowels may be omitted. Here are some examples.

I would like	tha <u>i</u>thela	tha'thela
to buy	na ago<u>ra</u>so	n'ago<u>ra</u>so
Thank you.	se efharis<u>to</u>	s'efharis<u>to</u>
I like it.	mu a<u>re</u>si	m'a<u>re</u>si
I like them.	mu a<u>re</u>sun	m'a<u>re</u>sun

Do you like …?	sas aresi …	s'aresi …
I will come.	tha ertho	tha'rtho
one boy	ena agori	en'agori

Words in Greek speech often run together. Articles that preceed nouns are pronounced with the noun. For example, the hotel, to ksenodohio is said as toxenodohio. This will be shown using an apostrophe in this book: to'ksenodohio.

Greetings

Let's start with common greetings. You are going to meet people so start with ka-li-me-ra. Certain phrases differ based on whether thay are said to one or more persons, or their usage in a formal or casual situation. As a visitor to Greece, it is more likely that you will use the formal phrases. Here are some other useful greetings:

Hello.	ya sas (pl, formal)	Γεια σας.
Hello.	ya su (singular)	Γεια σου.
Hello.	herete	χαίρετε
Good afternoon.	kalo apoyevma	Καλό απόγευμα.
Good morning.	kalimera	Καληλέρα.
Good day.	kalimera	Καληλέρα.
Good evening.	kalispera	Καλησπέρα.
Good night.	kalinihta	Καληνύχτα.
Goodbye.	athio	Αντίο.
Goodbye.	ya sas (pl, formal)	Γεια σας.
Goodbye.	ya su (singular)	Γεια σου.
How are you doing?	ti kanete (pl, formal)	Τι κάνετε;
How are you doing?	ti kanis (singular)	Τι κάνεις;
Are you well?	iste kala	Είστε καλά;
I am well.	ime kala	Είμαι καλά.
So so.	etsi ke etsi	Έτσι και έτσι.

Very well and you?	po<u>li</u> ka<u>la</u> e<u>sis</u>	Πολύ καλά εσείς;
Great! And you?	mia ha<u>ra</u> e<u>si</u>	Μια χαρά εσύ;
Very well .	po<u>li</u> ka<u>la</u>	Πολύ καλά.
You're welcome.	parakal<u>o</u>	Παρακαλώ.
Don't mention it. (it's nothing)	<u>ti</u>pota	Τίποτα.
America	ameri<u>ki</u>	Αμερική
Greece	el<u>a</u>tha	Ελλάδα
England	ang<u>li</u>a	Αγγλία
See you soon.	ta <u>leme</u> <u>sin</u>toma	Τα λέμε σύντομα.
See you later.	ta <u>leme</u> ar<u>go</u>tera	Τα λέμε αργότερα.
See you tomorrow.	ta <u>leme</u> <u>av</u>rio	Τα λέμε αύριο.
It's nice to meet you.	<u>hero</u> po<u>li</u>	Χαίρω πολύ.
What is your name?	pos sas <u>lene</u> (pl, formal)	Πώσ σας λένε;
What is your name?	pos se <u>lene</u> (singular)	Πώσ σε λένε;
My name is ...	me <u>lene</u> ...	Με λένε ...
Where are you staying?	pu <u>men</u>ete	Πού μένετε;
Are you Greek? (to a man)	<u>iste</u> <u>eli</u>nas	Είστε Έλληνας;
Are you Greek? (to a woman)	<u>ise</u> e<u>li</u>nitha	Είσαι Έλληνιδα;
I'm staying at ...	<u>meno</u> sto ...	Μένω στο ...
We're staying at ...	me<u>nume</u> sto ...	Μένουμε στο ...
Where do you work?	pu thul<u>ev</u>ete	Πού δουλεύετε;
What's up?	ti <u>yi</u>nete	Τι γίνεται;
Mr.	<u>ki</u>ria	Κύρια
Mrs.	ki<u>ri</u>a	Κυρία
Miss	thesp<u>inis</u>	Δεσποινίς

Notice the difference in which syllable is stressed in the Greek words for Mr. <u>ki</u>ria (first syllable) and Mrs. ki<u>ri</u>a (second syllable).

hero poli is a typical response when introduced to someone.

Nouns: Gender & Number (G)

Greek is a language glosa in which there are masculine, feminine and neuter nouns, as well as plural forms for each. The gender of a noun can typically be recognized by its ending.

Masculine: -os, -as

Feminine: -i, -a

Neuter: -i, -a, -o, -aki

In addition nouns have different endings depending on how they are used in a sentence. This is called declension. There are declension tables that show the patterns of nominative, accusative and genitive endings.

The nominative ending is used when the noun is the subject of the sentence. Nouns are shown in the nominative case in dictionaries. The accusative ending is used when the noun is the direct object of the sentence. The genitive ending is used when the noun shows possession of another object.

For singular nouns:

	Masculine	Feminine	Neuter
Nominative	-os	-i	-i
Accusative	-o	-i	-i
Genitive	-u	-is	-iu

For plural nouns:

	Masculine	Feminine	Neuter
Nominative	-i	-es	-ia

Accusative	-us	-es	-ia
Genitive	-on	-on	-ion

To show the different noun forms the following abbreviations will be used:

- ms - masculine singular
- mp - masculine plural
- fs - feminine singular
- fp - feminine plural
- ns - neuter singular
- np - neuter plural

Definite Articles

The definite article 'the' has different forms in Greek depending on the gender of the noun it precedes and also on the noun's usage in the sentence. There are also different singular and plural forms.

For singular articles:

	Masculine	Feminine	Neuter
Nominative	o	i	to
Accusative	ton	tin	to
Genitive	tu	tis	tu

For plural articles:

	Masculine	Feminine	Neuter
Nominative	i	i	ta
Accusative	tus	tis	ta
Genitive	ton	ton	ton

In this book all nouns are shown with their articles in the singular form. Say the nouns with their article as an aid to learning their gender.

Here are some examples of nouns with nominative endings and their definite articles. Proper names such as place names and names of people are also preceded by the appropriate definite article.

the road	o throm-os (ms)	ο δρόμος
the roads	i throm-i (mp)	η δρόμι
the mother	i miter-a (fs)	η μητέρα
the mothers	i miter-es (fp)	η μητέρες
the child	to peth-i (ns)	το παιδί
the children	ta peth-ia (np)	τα παιδία
Athens	i athina (fs)	η Αθήνα
Mr. Pappas	o kirios papas	ο κύριος Παππάς

Here are some examples of nouns with accusative endings and their definite articles:

I see the road.	vlepo to thromo	Βλέπω το δρόμο.
The street is long. (nom.)	o thromos ine makris	Ο δρόμος είναι μακρύς.
I see the street. (acc.)	vlepo to thromo	Βλέπω το δρόμο.

Here are some examples of nouns with genitive endings and their definite articles. Note the item possessed precedes the possessor.

the center of the city (city center)	to kendro tis polis (fs)	το κέντρο της πόλης
the man's wallet	portofoli tu anthrax	πορτοφόλι του άνδρα
This is Elena's mother.	avti ine i mitera tis elena	Αυτή είναι η μητέρα της Ελένα.
the woman's bag	tsanda tis yinekas	τσάντα της γυναίκας

13

Here are some examples of neuter nouns:

the hotel	to ksenodohio	το ξενοδοχείο
the restaurant	to estratorio	το εστιατόριο
the room	to thomatio	το δομάτιο

Here are some examples of feminine nouns:

the wife	i yineka	η γυναικά
the daughter	i kori	η κόρι
the mother	i mitera	η μητέρα

Some nouns have both masculine and feminine form.

friend	o filos (ms)	ο φίλος
friend	i fili (fs)	η φίλι
nurse	o nosokomos (ms)	ο νοσοκόμος
nurse	i nosokoma (fs)	η νοσοκόμα

Indefinite Articles

The indefinite article 'a' or 'an' agrees with the noun it precedes in gender and case. There is no plural for the indefinite article. The indefinite article is also the word for 'one'.

	Masculine	Feminine	Neuter
Nominative	enas	mia	ena
Accusative	enan	mia	ena
Genitive	enos	mias	enos

Here are some examples of the indefinite article:

a man	enas anthras	ένας άνδρας

a city	mia poli	μια πόλι
a bicycle	ena pothilato	ένα ποδίλατο

Finding Places

Here are some useful words for finding places. Start with 'Where is?' which in Greek is **pu ine**. This is followed by the article and the noun. Remember there are different articles for each gender. For example:

Where is the bathroom?	pu ine to banio	Πού είναι το μπάνιο;
Where is the restroom/toilet?	pu ine i tualeta	Πού είναι η τυαλέτα;
Where is the hotel?	pu ine to'ksenodohio	Πού είναι το ξενοδοχείο;
Where is the museum?	pu ine to musio	Πού είναι το μουσείο;
I want to go to the hotel.	thelo na pao sto'ksenodohio	Θέλω να πάο στο ξενοδοχείο.
Where is a telephone?	pu ine mia tilefono	Που είναι μια τηλέφωνο;
Where is ... street?	pu ine ... thromos	Που είναι ... δρόμος;

This is just a quick introduction, we'll go into directions in much more detail in a later section.

Conjunctions (G)

then	tote	τότε

although	an ke	αν και
and	ke	και
because	yati	Γιατί
but	ala	αλλά
or	i	η

For example:

steak and salad	brizola ke salata	μπριζόλα και σαλατά
the man and wife	o anthras ke i yineka	ο άνδρας και η γυναικά
here and there	etho ke eki	εδώ και εκεί
yes or no	ne i ohi	ναι ή όχι
open or closed	anixti i klisti	ανοιξτή ή κλειστή
left or right	thexia i aristera	δεξιά ή αριστερά

Expressing Needs and Wants

While travelling you may need to make requests for things that you want or need to do. To express a need for something you can use the phrase 'I want' thelo followed by a noun. To request some action use 'I want to ...' thelo na to connect with an action verb. The word na is equivalent to 'to' in English.

To be polite add parakalo. Alternatively, use 'I would like' tha ithela, which is typically said in a contracted form tha'thela. To say 'We want' use thelume followed by the word for the item in question.

Here are some examples of phrases to express needs and wants.

I want ...	thelo ...	Θέλω ...

We want …	thelume …	Θέλουμε …
I would like this.	tha ithela avto	Θα ήθελα αυτό.
I would like that.	tha thela ekino	Θα θελα εκείνο.
Do you want…?	thelete …	Θέλετε …;
Would you like…?	tha thelete …	Θα θέλετε …;
What do you want?	ti thelis	Τι θέλεις;
I prefer …	protimo …	Προτιμώ …
I like …	m'aresi …	Μου αρέσει …
I don't like …	then m'aresi …	Δεν μου αρέσει
Bring me …	ferte mu …	Φέρτε μου …
Give me …	thoste mu …	Δώτε μου …
Can you help me?	boris na me voithisis	Μπορείς να με βοήθεισις;
I need …	hriazome …	χρειάζομαι …
We want a room.	thelume ena thomatio	Θέλουμε ένα δωμάτιο
I want a taxi please.	thelo ena taxi parakalo	Θέλω ένα ταξί παρακαλώ.
I want to rent a taxi.	thelo na nikiaso ena taxi	Θέλω να νοικιάσω ένα ταξί.
I want to eat.	thelo na fao	Θέλω να φάω
We want to eat.	thelume na fame	Θέλουμε να φάμε.
I want to read a good book.	thelo na thiavaso ena kalo vivlio	Θέλω να διαβάσω ένα καλό βιβλίο
I want to drink.	thelo na pio	Θέλω να πιω
I want to buy …	thelo n'agoraso …	Θέλω να αγοράσω …
I want to pay.	thelo na pliroso	Θέλω να πληρώσω.
I want to write.	thelo na grapso	Θέλω να γράψω
I want to take the bus.	thelo na paro ena leoforio	Θέλω να πάρω ένα λεωφορείο.
I want to learn Greek.	thelo na matho elinika	Θέλω να μάθω ελληνικά.
I want to drink beer.	thelo na pio mia bira	Θέλω να πιω μια μπύρα.
Would you like to eat something?	tha thelete na fate kati	Θα θέλετε να φάτε κάτι;
I want to eat mousaka.	thelo na fao musaka	Θέλω να φάω μουσακά.

17

We want to go in the morning.	thelume na pao to proi	Θέλουμε να πάω το πρωί.
We want to order.	thelume na paragilete	Θέλουμε να παραγγείλετε.
I would like to eat something.	tha ithela na fao kati	Θα ήθελα να φάω κάτι.
Would you like to drink?	tha thelete na pite	Θα θέλετε να πιείτε;
I want to rent a car.	thelo na nikiaso ena avtokinito	Θέλω να νοικιάσω ένα αυτοκίνητο.
I want to withdraw money.	thelo na aposirun ta lefta	Θέλω να αποσύρουν τα λεφτά.
I want to exchange money.	thelo na antalaxo ta lefta	Θέλω να ανταλλάξω τα λεφτά.
I want to go to Crete.	thelo na pao stin kriti	Θέλω να πάω στην Κρήτη.
I am sorry	lipame	Λυπάμαι.
It is impossible	ine athinato	Είναι αδύνατο.
I need …	hriazome …	Χρειάζομε …
I prefer …	protimao …	Προτιμάω …
Yes please.	ne parakalo	Ναι παρακαλώ.
Thank you.	efharisto	ευχαριστώ.
No thanks.	ohi efharisto	Όχι ευχαριστώ.
Thanks a lot.	efharisto poli	Ευχαριστώ πολύ.
Many thanks. (1000 thanks)	hilia efharisto	Χίλια ευχαριστώ.
My pleasure.	efharistisi mu	Ευχαρίστηση μου.

Do you understand?

Now you need to respond to someone, did you understand what they said?

If you don't understand, reply ohi then katalaveno (no I don't understand. If you do understand, say katalaveno.

Here are some more useful phrases:

Do you understand English?	katala<u>ve</u>nete angli<u>ka</u>	Καταλαβαίνετε αγγλικά;
I don't understand.	then katala<u>ve</u>no	Δεν καταλαβαίνω.
I don't understand Greek.	then katala<u>ve</u>no elini<u>ka</u>	Δεν καταλαβαίνω ελληνικά.
Do you understand me?	me katala<u>ve</u>nis	Με καταλαβαίνεις;
I understand.	katala<u>ve</u>no	Καταλαβαίνω.
I speak a little Greek.	mil<u>ao</u> <u>li</u>go elini<u>ka</u>	Μιλάω λίγα Ελληνικά.
I don't speak Greek.	then mil<u>ao</u> elinika	Δεν πιλάω Ελληνικά.
I don't speak Greek well.	then mil<u>ao</u> ka<u>la</u> elini<u>ka</u>	Δεν πιλάω καλά Ελληνικά.
Are you American? (to a man)	<u>i</u>ste amerika<u>nos</u> (ms)	Ειστέ Αμερικανός;
I am American. (woman)	<u>i</u>me amerika<u>ni</u>tha (fs)	Είμαι Αμερικανίδα.
I am American. (man)	<u>i</u>me amerika<u>nos</u> (ms)	Είμαι Αμερικανός.
I am Greek. (man)	<u>i</u>me eli<u>nas</u> (ms)	Είμαι Έλληνας.
I am Greek. (woman)	<u>i</u>me eli<u>ni</u>tha (fs)	Είμαι Ελληνίδα.
Are you Greek? (to a man)	<u>i</u>ste eli<u>nas</u> (ms)	Ειστέ Ελληνίδα.
I'm from the States.	<u>i</u>me a<u>po</u> tin ameri<u>ki</u>	Είμαι από την Αμερική.
Where are you from? (formal)	a<u>po</u> pu is<u>te</u>	Από που ειστέ;
Where are you from? (informal)	a<u>po</u> pu <u>i</u>se	Από που είσαι;
I am from Greece.	<u>i</u>me a<u>po</u> tin e<u>la</u>tha	Είμαι από την Ελλάδα.
Do you speak English?	mil<u>a</u>te angli<u>ka</u>	Μιλάτε Αγγλικά;
Do you speak Greek?	mil<u>a</u>te elini<u>ka</u>	Μιλάτε Ελληνικά;
Does anyone speak	mil<u>ai</u> ka<u>nis</u> angli<u>ka</u>	Μιλάει κανείς

English?		αγγλικά;
And you?	ke es<u>is</u>	Και εσείς;
Please repeat	parak<u>a</u>lo epanalav<u>a</u>te	Παρακάλο επαναλαβάτε.
Slower please.	pio arg<u>a</u> paraka<u>lo</u>	Πιο αργά παρακαώ.
How do you pronounce this?	pos na apo<u>ther</u>i av<u>to</u>	Πώς να προφέρει αυτό;
What does it mean?	ti s<u>imeni</u> av<u>to</u>	Τι σημαίνει αυτό;
Write it down please.	<u>gra</u>pste to paraka<u>lo</u>	Γράψτε το παρακαλό.
I'm ok.	end<u>a</u>xi	Εντάξει.
Of course, sure.	vev<u>e</u>os	Βεβαίως.
Me too. (and I)	ke <u>e</u>go	Και εγώ.
Same here.	para<u>mi</u>os	Παραμοίως.
Only a little.	<u>mo</u>no <u>li</u>go	Μόνο λίγο.
Not very well.	<u>ohi po</u>li ka<u>la</u>	Όχι πολύ καλά.
I know.	ks<u>e</u>ro	Ξέρω.
I don't know.	then ks<u>e</u>ro	Δεν ξέρω.

Notice here that the words <u>ise</u> amerik<u>anos</u> can be spoken as a statement of fact or as a question. In English the word order is switched to indicate the question but in Greek you raise the intonation of your voice slightly towards the end of a question.

as a statement: You are American.	<u>ise</u> amerik<u>anos</u>	Είσαι Αμερικανός.
as a question: Are you American?	<u>ise</u> amerik<u>anos</u>	Είσαι Αμερικανός;

Questions and Answers?

You will be asking many questions when in Greece. We have already covered several words used in questions, let's look at some more. In written Greek a semi-colon is used as a question mark.

what?	ti	τι;
who?	pios (ms) pia (fs) pio (ns)	ποιος; ποιά; ποιό;
who? which ones?	pii (mp) pies (fp) pia (np)	ποιί; ποιές; ποιά;
when?	pote	πότε;
why?	yati	γιατί;
how?	pos	πώς;
how much?	posos (ms) posi (fs) poso (ns)	πόσος; πόσι; πόσο;
how many?	posi (mp) poses (fp) posa (np)	πόσι; πόσες; πόσα;
where?	pu	πού;
which?	poio	ποιο;

Now let's go over some questions erotisis and some answers apandisis.

What happened?	ti sinevi	Τι συνέβη;
What's this?	ti ine avto	Τι είναι αυτό;
Who is it?	pios ine	Ποιος είναι;
What do you want?	ti thelete	Τι θέλετε;
Where are you from? (informal)	apo pu ise	από πού είσαι;
Where do you live in America?	pu menete stin ameriki	Πού μένετε στην Αμερική;
We live in America.	menume stin ameriki	Μένουμε στην Αμερική.
I'm from ...	ime apo to ...	Είμαι από το ...
We are from ...	imaste apo to ..	Είμαστε από το ...
Do you live here?	menete etho	Μένετε εδώ;
Where do you	pu thulevete	Που δουλεύετε;

work?		
Where is the restaurant?	pu ine to estiatorio	Που είναι το εστιατόριο;
Where is the room?	pu ine to thomatio	Που είναι το δομάτιο;
Where are we going?	pu pame	Πού πάμε;
I am going to Athens.	pao stin athina	Πάω στην Αθήνα.
We are going to the restaurant.	pame sto estatorio	Πάμε στο εστιατόριο.
It's here.	ine etho	Είναι εδώ.
It's there.	ine eki	Είναι εκεί.
What's your name? (informal)	pos se leme	Πώς σε λέμε;
What's your name? (formal)	pos sas leme	Πώς σας λέμε;
My name is ...	me leme ...	Με λέμε ...
What time is it? (literally: what is the hour?)	ti ora ine	Τι ώρα είναι;
What don't I understand?	ti then katavaleno	Τι δεν καταλαβαίνω;
When are we going?	otan pame	όταν πάμε;
When is breakfast?	otan ine proino	όταν είναι πρωινό;
How much per person?	poso kani to atomo	πόσο κάνει το άτομο
How much per night?	poso kani to vrathia	πόσο κάνει το βραδιά
How do you say ... in Greek?	pos lene ... sta elinika	Πώς λένε ... στα Ελληνικά;

Negation (G)

To express the negative the words **the(n)** or **mi(n)** immediately before the verb.

Here are examples of their usage:

I don't want to go.	the thelo na pao	Δέ θέλω να παώ.
I don't know.	then ksero	Δεν ξέρω.
There's no water.	then iparhi nero	Δεν υπάρχει νερό.
I don't like …	then m'aresi …	Δεν μου αρέσει …

Adjectives (G)

In Greek, the adjective always comes before the noun, as in English. The adjective must match the noun in gender (masculine, feminine or neuter) and number (singular or plural) with the following endings. For adjectives that end with -os.

For singular nouns:

	Masculine	Feminine	Neuter
Nominative	-os	-i	-o
Accusative	-o	-i	-o
Genitive	-u	-is	-u

For plural nouns:

	Masculine	Feminine	Neuter
Nominative	-i	-es	-a
Accusative	-us	-es	-a
Genitive	-on	-on	-on

Here are some examples of nouns with matching adjectives.

The big man	o megalos anthros (ms)	ο μεγάλος άνδρας
the big women	i megales yinekes (fp)	οι μεγάλες γυναίκες
the good food	to kalo fayito	το καλό φαγητό
the deep sea	i vathia thalasa (fs)	η βαθιά θάλασσα
the open book	to anihto vivlio (ns)	το ανοιχτό βιβλίο
the open books	to anihta vivlia (np)	τα ανοιχτά βιβλία
the cold water	to krio nero (ns)	το κρύο νερό
some wine	ligo krasi (ns)	λίγο κρασί
some beer	ligi bira (fs)	λίγι μπύρα

For adjectives that end with -is .

For singular nouns:

	Masculine	Feminine	Neuter
Nominative	-os	-ia	-i
Accusative	-i	-ia	-i
Genitive	-iu	-ias	-iu

For plural nouns:

	Masculine	Feminine	Neuter
Nominative	-i	-es	-ia
Accusative	-ius	-es	-ia
Genitive	-on	-on	-on

Here are some adjectives in their masculine, singular forms:

big	megalos	μεγάλος
bad	kakos	κακός
beautiful	omorfos	όμορφος
good	kalos	καλός
nice	oreos	ωραίος
small	mikros	μικρός
easy	evkolos	εύκολος
quick	grighoros	γρήγορος

slow	argos	αργός
warm	zestos	ζεστός
hot	kavto	καυτό
cold	krios	κρύος
hard	skliros	σκληρός
soft	malakos	μαλακός
interesting	enthiaferon	ενδιαφέρων
full	yematos	γεμάτος
empty	athinos	αδινός
deep	vathis	βαθύς
heavy	varis	βαρύς
light	elafris	ελαφρύς
long	makris	μακρύς
short	kondos	κοντός
difficult	thiskolos	δυσκολός
open	anihtos	ανοιχτός
closed	klistos	κλειστός
cheap	ftinos	φτηνός
expensive	akriva	ακριβά
new	neos	νέος
old	palios	παλιός
clean	katharos	καθαρός
dirty	vromikos	βρώμικος
tall	psilos	ψηλός
short	kondo	κοντό

Adjectives can be turned into comparatives 'better' by adding the word **pio** meaning 'more' after the adjective. For example:

better	pio kalos	πιό καλός
colder	pio krio	πιό κρύο
warmer	pio zestos	πιό ζεστός
newer	pio neos	πιό νέος
nearer	pio konda	πιο κοντά
bigger, larger	pio megalos	πιό μεγάλος
heavier	pio varia	πιό βαριά
higher	pio psilo	πιό ψηλό
later	pio arga	πιό αργά

more interesting	pio enthiaferon	πιό ενδιαφέρων
smaller	pio mikros	πιό μικρός
more slowly	pio arga	πιό αργά

There are also these words for comparison:

smaller	mikroteros	μικρότερος
the smallest	o mikroteros	ο μικρότερος
bigger, larger	megaliteros	μεγαλύτερος
the biggest	o megaliteros	ο μεγαλύτερος
the nearest	o kondinoteros	ο κοντινότερος

Commonly Used Words

Here some commonly used words.

inside	mesa	πέσα
outside	exo	έξω
all, everything	ola	όλα
also	episis	επίσις
at	stis	στις
but	ala	αλλά
maybe, possibly	isos	Ίσος
nothing	tipota	τίποτα
never	pote	Ποτέ
nobody, no-one	kaneis	κανείς
only	mono	μόνο
forbidden	apagorevete	απαγορεύεται
some (when referring to money, etc)	merika	μερικά
some	ligo (ms), ligi (fs), ligo (ns)	λίγο
something	kati	κάτι
sometimes	kapote	κάποτε

soon	sindoma	σύντομα
this	av<u>to</u> (ns)	αυτό
that	e<u>ki</u>no (ns)	εκείνο
possible	thina<u>to</u>	δυνατό
naturally, of course	fisi<u>ka</u>	φυσικά

Numbers

number	arith<u>mos</u>	αριθμός
0	mi<u>then</u>	μηδέν
1	<u>e</u>na	ένα
2	<u>thi</u>o	δυο
3	<u>tri</u>a	τρία
4	<u>te</u>sera	τέσσερα
5	<u>pen</u>de	πέντε
6	<u>e</u>xi	έξι
7	ep<u>ta</u>	επτά
8	ok<u>to</u>	οκτώ
9	eni<u>a</u>	εννιά
10	<u>the</u>ka	δέκα
11	<u>en</u>teka	έντεκα
12	th<u>o</u>heka	δώδεκα
13	theka-<u>tri</u>a	δεκαρεια
14	theka-<u>te</u>sara	δεκατέσσερα
15	theka-<u>pen</u>de	δεκαπέντε
16	theka-<u>e</u>xi	δεκαέξι
17	theka-ep<u>ta</u>	δεκαεπτά
18	theka-ok<u>to</u>	δεκαοχτώ
19	theka-eni<u>a</u>	δεκαεννέα
20	<u>i</u>kosi	είκοσι
21	<u>i</u>kosi ena	είκοσι ένα
30	tri<u>an</u>da	τριάντα
40	sar<u>an</u>da	σαράντα
50	pen<u>in</u>da	πενήντα
60	ex<u>in</u>da	εξήντα

70	evthominda	εβδομήτα
80	okthonda	ογδόντα
90	eneninda	ενενήτα
100	ekato	εκατό
200	thiakosia	διακόσια
300	triakosia	τριακόσια
400	tetrakosia	τετρακόσια
1000	hilia	χίλια
2000	thio hiliades	δύο χιλιάδες

Now for the ordinals:

first	prota	πρώτα
second	thefteros	δεύτερος
third	tritos	τρίτος
fourth	tetartos	τέταρτος
fifth	pemptos	πέμπτος
sixth	ektos	έκτος
seventh	evthomos	έβδομος
eighth	ogdu	όγδοο
ninth	enatos	ένατος
tenth	thekatos	δέκατος

Time

To ask 'What time is it?' you say ti ora ine. A minute is lepto and the plural minutes is leptos. Here are all the hour numbers:

The word mia is used instead of ena for one o'clock.

The word tris is used instead of tria for three o'clock.

To say the half hour, add ke misi after the hour. For example: 8:30 is mia ke misi.

To say quarter past the hour, add ke t̲e̲t̲arto after the hour (literally: the hour and a quarter). For example: quarter past two is t̲h̲io ke t̲e̲t̲arto.

To say quarter to the hour, add pa̲r̲a̲ t̲e̲t̲arto after the hour. For example: quarter to one is m̲i̲a̲ pa̲r̲a̲ t̲e̲t̲arto

To say minutes past the hour, use 'hour ke minute'. For example:

ten past one m̲i̲a̲ ke t̲h̲e̲ka

twenty past twelve t̲h̲o̲theka ke i̲k̲osi

To say minutes before the hour, use 'hour pa̲r̲a̲ minute'. For example:

five to one m̲i̲a̲ pa̲r̲a̲ pe̲n̲de

twenty to twelve t̲h̲o̲theka pa̲r̲a̲ i̲k̲osi

Here are some examples:

It's three o'clock.	i̲n̲e tris	Είναι τρεις.
What time is it?	ti o̲r̲a i̲n̲e	Τι ώρα είναι;
What time?	ti o̲r̲a	Τι ώρα;
What time does it start?	ti o̲r̲a arh̲i̲zi	Τι ώρα αρχίζει;
At 8:00 p.m.	stis okt̲o̲ mi mi	Στις οκτώ μ.μ.
What time does it end?	ti o̲r̲a teli̲o̲ni	Τι ώρα τελειώνει;
Do you have the time?	m̲i̲pos e̲h̲ete o̲r̲a	Πήπος έχετε ώρα;
At five o'clock.	stis pe̲n̲de i o̲r̲a	Στις πένδε η ώρα.
I want to go in the morning.	th̲e̲lo na pa̲o̲ to pro̲i̲	Θέλω να πάω το πρωί.
I have 30 minutes.	e̲h̲o tria̲n̲da lep̲t̲a	Έχω τριάντα λεπτά.
When will the train go?	po̲te tha pa̲i̲ to treno	Πότε θα πάει το τρένο;
At one.	stis m̲i̲a	Στις μία.
At eight.	stis oct̲o̲	Στις οκτώ.

Other useful words:

after	meta	μετά
before	prin	πριν
noon, midday	to mesimeri (ns)	μεσημέρι
hour	i ora (fs)	όρα
minute	to lepto (ns)	λεπτό
second	to thefterolepto (ns)	δευτερόλεπτο
calendar	to imeroloyio (ns)	ημερολόγιο
clock, watch	to roloi (ns)	ρολόι
date	i imerominia (fs)	ημερομηνία
day	i mera (fs)	μέρα
time	o hronos (ms)	χρόνος
today	simera	σήμερα
every day	kathe mera	κάθε μέρα
morning	to proi (ns)	πρωί
afternoon	to apoyevma (ns)	απόγευμα
tonight	apopse	απόψε
yesterday	htes	χτες
day before yesterday	prohtes	προχτές
evening	to vrathi (ns)	βράδυ
night	i nihta (fs)	νύχτα
tomorrow	avrio	αύριο
tomorrow evening	avrio vrathi (ns)	αύριο βράδυ
timetable	hrono-thiagramma	χρονοδιάγραμμα
year	to etos (ns)	έτος
year	hronos	χρόνος
this year	fetos	φέτος
last year	persi	πέρυσι
next year	hronu	χρόνου
month	to mina (ns)	μήνα
next month	epomeno mina	επόμενο μήνα
not yet	ohi akomi	όχι ακόμη
immediately	amesos	αμέσως
now	tora	τώρα
Wait!	perimene	Περίμενε!
Just a minute.	miso lepto	Μισό επτό.

In half an hour.	se misi ora	Σε μισή ώρα.
week	i evthomatha (fs)	εβδομάδα
fortnight	to thekapenthimeo (ns)	δεκαπενθήμεο
weekend	to savatokiriako (ns)	Σαββατοκύριακο
while	eno	ενώ
Happy New Year. (literally: good year)	kali hronia	Καλή χρονιά.
late	arga	αργά
later	argotera	αργότερα
early	noris	νωρίς
exactly	akrivos	ακριβώς
maybe	isos	ίσως

And now for some phrases.

Come early.	erhome noris	Έρχομαι νωρίς.
What time is it?	ti ora ine	Τι ώρα είναι;
It's early.	ine noris	Είναι νωρίς.
Today at 6:15	simera stis exi ke tetarto	Σήμερα στις έξι και τέταρτο.
Tomorrow afternoon	avrio to apoyevma	Αύριο το απόγευμα.
Yesterday afternoon	hthes to apoyevma	Χθες το απόγευμα.
What time is breakfast?	ti ora ine to proino	Τι ώρα είναι το πρωινό;
What time does it open/close?	ti ora aniyi / klini	Τι ώρα ανοίγει / κλείνει;

Days and Seasons

You'll need to know the days of the week **evtho<u>ma</u>tha** at some point.

Sunday	kiria<u>ki</u>	Κυριακή
Monday	thef<u>te</u>ra	Δευτέρα
Tuesday	<u>tri</u>ti	Τρίτη
Wednesday	te<u>tar</u>ti	Τετάρτη
Thursday	<u>pe</u>mpti	Πέμπτη
Friday	paras<u>ke</u>vi	Παρασκευή
Saturday	<u>sav</u>ato	Σάββατο

And now for some phrases.

On Thursday	tin <u>pe</u>mpdi	την Πέμπτη
Saturday night	<u>sav</u>ato <u>vra</u>thi	Σάββατο βράδυ
Next week	tin e<u>po</u>meni evtho<u>ma</u>tha	την επόμενη εβδομάδα

Here are the seasons.

season	i e<u>po</u>hi (fs)	εποχή
spring	i <u>a</u>nixi (fs)	άνοιξη
summer	to kalo<u>ke</u>ri (ns)	καλοκαίρι
autumn, fall	to fthi<u>no</u>poro (ns)	φθινόπωρο
winter	o hi<u>mo</u>nas (ms)	χειμώνας

Months of the year <u>etos</u>.

January	yanu<u>a</u>rios	Ιανουάριος
February	fevru<u>a</u>rios	Φεβρουάριος
March	<u>mar</u>tios	Μάρτιος
April	a<u>pri</u>los	Απρίλος
May	<u>ma</u>ios	Μάιος
June	<u>yu</u>nios	Ιούνιος

July	yulios	Ιούλιος
August	avgustos	Αύγουστος
September	septemvrios	Σεπτέμβριος
October	octovrios	Οκτώβριος
November	noemvrios	Νοέμβριος
December	dekemvrios	Δεκέμβριος

Chatting about the weather keros.

Summer is very hot.	to kalokeri ine poli zesto	Το καλοκαίρι είναι πολύ ζεστό.
Beautiful weather.	oreos keros	Οραίος καιρός.
Beautiful day.	ine mia oreos mera	Είναι μια οραίος μέρα.
It is hot in July.	kani zesti ton yulios	Κάνει ζέστη τον Ιούλιος.
It is cold.	kani krio	Κάνει κρύο.

Telephones and Such

Everyone has a mobile phone kinito these days, but you will likely need these words to help you deal with modern communications and technology for the traveller.

area code	o kothikas (ms)	κώδικας
battery	i bataria (fs)	μπαταρία
battery charger	to fortisti batarias (ns)	φορτιστή μπαταρίας
camera	i kamera (fs)	κάμερα
cellphone	to kinito (tilefono) (ns)	κινητό (τηλέφωνο)
computer	o ipoloyistis (ms)	υπολογιστής
computer disk	o thiskos ipologisti (ms)	δίσκος υπολογιστή
converter	to metatropeas (ns)	μετατροπέας
dial, press (v)	kalesete	καλέσετε

download (v)	thiavivazo	διαβιβάζω
edit	epexergasia	επεξεργασία
electricity	i ilektrismos (fs)	ηλεκτρισμός
email	to email (ns)	εμαιλ
file	to arhio (ns)	αρχείο
headphones	ta akustika (np)	ακουστικά
Internet	thiathiktio	διαδίκτυο
international	pangosmios	παγκόσμιος
keyboard	to pliktrologio (ns)	πληκτρολόγιο
loudspeaker	to megafono (ns)	μεγάφωνο
login name	to onoma sinthesis (ns)	όνομα σύνδεσης
password	o kothikos prosvasis (ms)	κωδικός πρόσβασης
message	to minima (ns)	μήνυμα
mouse	to pondiki (ns)	ποντίκι
personal computer	prosopikos ipoloyistis	προσωπικός υπολογιστής
phonecard	to tilekarta (ns)	τηλεκάρτα
photograph	i fotografia (fs)	φωτογραφία
plug (electric)	to priza (ns)	πρίζα
printer	o ektiposis (ms)	εκτυπωτής
print (v)	ektiposi tipono	εκτύπωτη
save (v)	sozo	σώζω
scanner	o sarotis (ms)	σαρωτής
screen	i othoni (fs)	οθόνη
software	to logismiko (ns)	λογισμικό
switch	o thiakoptis (ms)	διακόπτης
telephone	to tilefono (ns)	τηλέφωνο
telephone book	o tilefonikos othigos (ms)	Τηλεφωνικός οδηγός
telephone box	o tilefonikos thalamus (ms)	τηλεφωνικός θάλαμος
telephone call	to tilefonima (ns)	τηλεφώνημα
telephone number	o arithmos tilefonu (ms)	αριθμός τηλεφώνου
telephone operator	o tilefonias (ms)	τηλεφωνίας

voice	i foni (fs)	φωνή
voice mail	to tilefoniti (ns)	τηλεφωνητή
yellow pages	hrisos othigos	Χρυσός Οδηγός
wireless	asirmatos	ασύρματος

And now for some phrases.

Is ... there?	ine o/i ... eki	Είναι ο/η ... εκεί;
May I speak with ... ?	boro na milite me ton ...	Μπορώ να μιλήσω με τον ...;
Here is the number.	etho ine to numero	Εθό είναι το νούμερο
Don't hang up.	min klisete	Μην κλείσετε.
Hello?	embros	Εμπρός;
Give me a phone call.	those mu ena tilefonima	Δώσε μου ένα τηλεφώνημα.
What's your number?	ti ine o arithmos sas	Τι είναι ο αριθμός σας;
My number is ...	o arithmos mu ine ...	Ο αριθμός μου είναι ...

Verbs (G)

It's time for an introduction to Greek verbs. Active verbs are those that cause an action on someone or something else. Passive verbs are those that cause an action on the subject. All active verbs have an -o ending. All passive verbs have a -me ending. All verbs as listed in the first person singular form in the same manner as found in dictionaries.

Let's start by looking at the present tense where the verbs are modified according to number, that is singular or plural, and gender. Each verb has a stem (or root) followed by a suffix that is differs by number, and gender.

This table shows the present tense conjugation of the active verb 'I write'.

I write	grafo	γράφω

You write	grafis	γράφεις
He/she/it writes	grafi	γράφει
We write	grafume	γράφουμε
You write	grafete	γράφετε
They write	grafun	γράφουν

This table shows the present tense conjugation of the active verb 'I want'.

I want	thelo	θέλω
You want	thelis	θέλεις
He/she/it wants	theli	θέλει
We want	thelume	θέλουμε
You want	thelete	θέλετε
They want	thelun(e)	θέλουν

Here is the present tense conjugation for the passive verb 'I am':

I am	ime	είμαι
You are	ise	είσαι
He/she/it is	ine	είναι
We are	imaste	είμαστε
You are	iste	είστε
They are	ine	είναι

Present Tense Active Verbs

Here is the list of active verbs.

I agree	simfono	συμφωνώ
I allow	epitrepo	επιτρέπω
I answer	apando	απαντώ
I arrive	ftano	φτάνω
I ask (question)	roto	ροτό
I ask (for	zito	ζητώ

something)		
I begin, start	ksekino	ξεκινώ
I believe	pistevo	πιστεύω
I bring	ferno	φέρνω
I buy	agorazo	αγοράζω
I can	boro	μπορώ
I change	alaxo	αλλάξω
I choose	thialego	διαλέγω
I close	klino	κλείνω
I continue	snehizo	συνεχίζω
I count	metrao	μετράω
I do	kano	κάνω
I dislike	antipatho	αντιπαθώ
I drink	pino	Πίνω
I drive	othigo	οδηγώ
I eat	troo	τρώω
I end	telioso	τελειώσω
I enter	beno	μπαίνω
I fill	yemizo	γεμίζω
I find	vrisko	βρίσκω
I fly	petao	πετάω
I follow	akolutho	ακολουθώ
I forget	ksehno	ξεχνώ
I get	perno	παίρνω
I give	thino	δίνω
I go	piyeno	πηγαίνω
I have	eho	έχω
I hear	akuo	ακούω
I help	voitho	βοήθω
I hire	nikiazo	νικιάζω
I know	ksero	ξέρω
I laugh	yelo	γελώ
I learn	matheno	μαθαίνω
I leave	afino	αφήνω
I please	areso	αρέσω
I live, stay	meno	μένω
I look for	psahno	ψάχνω
I lose	hano	χάνω
I love	agapo	αγαπώ

I make	ftiahno	φτιάχνω
I meet	sinando	συναντώ
I open	anigo	ανοίγω
I order (food)	paragelno	παραγγέλνω
I owe	hrostao	χρωστάω
I park (a car)	stathmevo	σταθμεύω
I pay	plirono	πληρώνω
I prefer	protimo	προτιμώ
I prepare	etimazo	ετοιμάζω
I must	prepi	πρέπει
I read	thiavaso	διάβασω
I receive	lavo	λάβω
I return	epistrefo	επιστρέφω
I say	leo	λέω
I see	vlepo	βλέπω
I sell	pulo	πουλώ
I send	stelno	στέλνω
I shout	fonazo	φωνάζω
I shut	klino	κλείνω
I sign	ipografo	υπογράφω
I speak	milo / milao	μιλω / μιλάω
I spend (time)	perno	παίρνω
I stay	meno	μένω
I swim	kolibo	κολυμπώ
I telephone	tilefono	τηλέφωνο
I think	nomizo	νομίζω
I touch	agizo	αγγίζω
I travel	taxithevo	ταξιδεύω
I try	prospatho	προσπαθώ
I understand	katalaveno	καταλαβαίνω
I use	hrisimopio	χρησιμοποιώ
I wait	perimeno	περιμένω
I walk	perpato	περπατώ
I want	thelo	Θέλω
I wear	forao	φοράω
I work	thulevo	δουλεύω
I write	grafo	γράφω
I welcome	kalosorizo	καλωσορίζω

Present Tense Passive Verbs

Here is the list of passive verbs.

I accept	apothekome	αποδέχομαι
I am	ime	είμαι
I am glad	herome	χαίρομαι
I am in a hurry	viazome	βιάζομαι
I am sorry	lipame	λυπάμαι
I borrow	thanizome	δανιζείζομαι
I come	erhome	έρχομαι
I feel	esthanome	αισθάνομαι
I am lost	hanome	χάνομαι
I land	prosyionete	προσγειώνεται
I need	hriazome	χρειάζομαι
I remember	thimame	θυμάάμαι
I share	mirazome	μοιράζομαι
I sit	kathome	κάθομαι
I sleep	kimame	κοιμάμαι
I stand	stekome	στέκομαι
I take off	apoyionete	απογειώνεται
I think	skeptome	σκέπτομαι
I visit	episkeptome	επισκέπτομαι

Verbs must agree with their subject in number and person. See the verb tables for details on how key verbs are conjugated. Here are some examples.

The train is coming.	to treno ehete	Το τρένο έρχεται.
My wife wants to go.	i yineka mu theli na pai	Η γυναίκα μου θέλει να πάει.
The women are going.	i yinekas pane	Οι γυναίκες πάνε.
I am eating.	ego troo	Εγώ τρώω.
My husband is eating.	o anthras mu troi	Ο άνδρας μου τρώει.
The girls are eating.	ta koritsia trone	Το κορίτσια τρώνε.

mu aresi

The word 'I please' areso is very commonly used in the third person form. The singular is **mu aresi** (it pleases me) and the plural is **mu aresun** (they please me).

Singular:

I like (single item)	mu aresi	μου αρέσει
You like	su aresi	σού αρέσει
He/she/it likes	tu/tis/tu aresi	του/τις/του αρέσει
We like	mas aresi	μας αρέσει
You like	sas aresi	σας αρέσει
They like	tus aresi	τους αρέσει

Plural:

I like (many items)	mu aresun	μου αρέσουν
You like	su aresun	σού αρέσουν
He/she/it likes	tu/tis/tu aresun	του/τις/του αρέσουν
We like	mas aresun	μας αρέσουν
You like	sas aresun	σας αρέσουν
They like	tus aresun	τους αρέσουν

Here some examples of its usage:

I like this.	mu aresi avto	Μου αρέσει αυτό.
I like it a a lot.	mu aresi poli	Μου αρέσει πολύ.
Do you like Greece?	sas aresi i elatha	Σας αρέσει η Ελλάδα;
I like them.	mu aresun	Μου αρέσουν.

The following verb tenses are described in this book:

- Present tense
- Past tense

- Future tense

- Imperative. This is a request or command. For example, 'Shut the door!'

This chapter has introduced you to the present tense, the other tenses will be discussed later.

At the Hotel

When staying at a hotel **ksenodohio** you will need these words:

address	i thiefthinsi (fs)	διεύθυνση
air conditioning	o klimatismos (ms)	κλιματισμός
air conditioner	to klimatistiko (ns)	κλιματιστικό
balcony	to balkoni (ns)	μπαλκόνι
bathroom	to banio (ns)	μπάνιο
bed	to krevati (ns)	κρεβάτι
bed sheet	to sendoni (ns)	σεντόνι
blanket	i kuverta (fs)	κουβέρτα
city	i poli (fs)	πόλι
confirmation	epiveveosi	επιβεβαίωσι
corridor	o thiathromos (ms)	διάδρομο
country	i hora (fs)	χώρα
couple	to zevgari (ns)	ζευγάρι
dining room	i trapezaria (fs)	τραπεζαρία
double bed	to thiplo krivati (ns)	διπλό κρεβάτι
double room	to thiplo thomatio (ns)	διπλό δωμάτιο
down	kato	κάτω
dry cleaning	stegno katharisma	στεγνό καθάρισμα
elevator, lift	to anelkistiras (ns)	ανελκυστήρας
elevator, lift	to asanser (ns)	ασανσέρ
electricity	elektrismos	ηλεκτρισμός
first name	to mikro onoma (ns)	μικρό όνομα
last name	to epiteto (ns)	επίθετο
fan (electric)	o amenistiras (ms)	ανεμιστήρας
haircut	to kurema (ns)	κούρεμα

hairdresser	o komotis (ms)	κομμωτής
hair dryer	to sesuar (ns)	σεσουάρ
hostel	o zenonas (ns)	ζενώνας
hotel	to ksenodohio (ns)	ξενοδοχείο
hot water	to zesto nero (ns)	ζεστό νερό
inn	to pandohio (ns)	πανδοχείο
key	to klithi (ns)	κλειδί
lamp	i lampa (fs)	λάμπα
lightbulb	glombos	γλόμπος
manager	o thiefthindis (ms)	διευθυντής
matress	to stroma (ns)	στρώμα
name	to onoma (ns)	όνομα
nationality	ipiko-otita	υπηκοότητα
noise	o thorivos (ms)	θόρυβος
pen	to stilo (ns)	στυλό
pillow	to maxilari (ns)	μαξιλάρι
plug (electric)	to fisa (ns)	φίσα
quiet	isiha	ήσυχα
refrigerator	to psiyio (ns)	ψυγείο
remote control	tilehiristirio	τηλεχειριστήριο
room	to thomatio (ns)	δωμάτιο
reservation	i kratisi (fs)	κράτηση
shower	to duz (ns)	ντους
signature	i ipografo (fs)	υπογράφω
single	mono	μονό
sink	to nerohitis (ns)	νεροχύτης
soap	to sapuni (ns)	σαπούνι
socket (electric)	to ilektriki prizi (ns)	ηλεκτρική πρίζα
stairs	i skala (fs)	σκάλα
swimming pool	i pisina (fs)	πισίνα
tap, faucet	i vrisi (fs)	βρύση
towel	i petseta (fs)	πετσέτα
up, upstairs	epano	επάνω
washing machine	to plintirio (ns)	πλυντήριο
zip code	T.K. tahithromikos tomeas	ταχυδρομικός τομέας

And now for some phrases that you can use.

I have made a reservation. .	eho kani kratisi	Έχω κάνει κράτηση.
Can you recommend a cheap hotel?	borite na mu protinete ena fthino ksenodohio	Μπορείτε να προτείνετε ένα φτηνό ξενοδοχείο;
What is your name? (Lit: how do they call you?)	pos sas lene	Πώσ σας λένε;
My name is ... (I am called ...)	me lene ...	Με λένε ...
Do you have a room with a shower?	ehete ena thomatio me duz	Έχετε ένα δωμάτιο με ντους;
Do you have a double room for one night?	ehete ena thiplo thomatio ya mia nihta	Έχετε ένα διπλό δωμάτιο για μία νύχτα;
We would like a room.	thelume ena thomatio	Θέλουμε ένα δωμάτιο.
Yes, we have a room.	ne ehume ena thomatio	Ναι έχουμε ένα δωμάτιο.
For one night.	ya mia nihta	για μία νύχτα.
How much is (costs) the room?	poso kostizi to thomatio	Πόσο κοστίζι το δομάτιο;
I want a room.	thelo ena thomatio	Θέλω ένα δωμάτιο.
With two beds.	me thio krevatia	Με δύο κρεβάτια.
With a double bed.	me ena thiplo krevati	Με ένα διπλό κρεβάτι.
Is there air-conditoning?	eki klimatismu	Εκεί κλιματισμού;
How long will you be staying?	poso kero tha minete	Πόσο καιρό θα μείνετε.
Sign here.	ipografste etho	Υπογράψτε εδώ.
What is the room number?	poios ine o arithmos tu thomatiu	Ποιος είναι ο αριθμός του δωματίου;
Your room number is ...	ine o arithmos tu thomatiu sas ine	Ο αριθμός του δωματίου σας

43

	...	είναι ...
Here is your key.	e<u>tho</u> <u>ine</u> to kli<u>thi</u> sas	Εδώ είναι το κλειδί σας.
Do not disturb.	min enoh<u>lite</u>	Μην ενοχλείτε.
Come in.	pe<u>ra</u>ste	Περάστε.
We are leaving tomorrow.	<u>fey</u>gume <u>av</u>tio	Φεύγουμε αύριο.
I am leaving today.	<u>fey</u>go <u>si</u>mera	Φεύγω σήμερα.
Can I have the bill?	bo<u>ro</u> na <u>e</u>ho ton logaria<u>smo</u>	Μπορώ να έχω το λογαριασμό;
The telephone does not work.	to ti<u>le</u>fono then thu<u>le</u>vi	Το τηλέφωνο δεν δουλεύει
Where is a good restaurant?	pu <u>ine</u> <u>e</u>na ka<u>lo</u> estia<u>to</u>rio	Που είναι ένα καλό εστιατόριο;
There is a good restaurant here.	p<u>par</u>hi <u>e</u>na ka<u>lo</u> estia<u>to</u>rio e<u>tho</u>	Υπάρχει ένα καλό εστιατόριο εδώ.

Directions

You are certainly going to explore Athens **Athina** on a trip to Greece. To help you find places and get some directions, let's start with some commands that you may hear:

go (vi)	<u>pi</u>yene	πήγαινε
take (vi)	<u>pa</u>rete	πάρετε
turn (vi)	<u>strip</u>ste	στρίψτε

Now for some other useful words:

address	i thie<u>fthin</u>si (fs)	διεύθυνση
Acropolis	i a<u>kro</u>poli (fs)	Ακρόπολη
avenue	i leo<u>fo</u>ros (fs)	λεωφόρος
at	se	σε
behind	<u>pi</u>so a<u>po</u>	πίσω από
excuse me	sig<u>no</u>mi	συγγνώμη
where?	pu	Που;

direction	i katefunsi (fs)	κατεύφυνση
airport	to erothromio (ns)	αεροδρόμιο
antiquities	i arheotites	αρχαιότητες
corner	i gonia (fs)	γωνία
church	i eklisia (fs)	εκκλησία
Plaka	plaka	Πλάκα
police station	to astinomiko tmima (ns)	αστινομικό τμήμα
train	to treno (ns)	τρένο
bridge	i yefira (fs)	γέφυρα
building	to ktirio (ns)	κτίριο
bus stop	i stasi leoforio (fs)	στάσι λεωφορείο
cathedral	i mitropoli (fs)	
castle	to kastro (ns)	κάστρο
center	to kendro (ns)	κέντρο
city center	to kendro tis polis (ns)	κέντρο της πόλης
closed	klistos	κλειστός
coffee shop	to kafenio (ns)	καφενείο
entrance	i isothos (fs)	είσοδος
exit	i exothos (fs)	έξοδος
fortress	to frurio (ns)	φρούριο
guide	o othigos (ms)	οδηγός
guidebook	o turistikos othigos (ns)	τουριστικ οδηγός
harbor	to limani (ns)	λιμάνι
island	to nisi (ns)	νησί
sidewalk	to pezothromio (ns)	πεζοδρόμιο
monument	to minio (ns)	μνηνείο
museum	to musio (ns)	μουσείο
office	to grafio (ns)	γραφείο
one way	enas tropos	ένας τρόπος
open	aniktos	ανοικτός
plaza, town square	i platia (fs)	πλατεία
post office	to tahithromio (ns)	ταχυδρομείο
restaurant	to estiatorio (ns)	εστιατόριο
road	o thromos (ms)	δρόμος
ruins	ta eripia (np)	τα ερείπια

port	to limani (ns)	λιμάνι
stadium	to stathio (ns)	στάδιο
station	o stathmos (ms)	σταθμός
store	to katastima (ns)	Κατάστημα
street	o thromos (ms)	δρόμος
street	othos	οδός
subway	to metro (ns)	μετρό
subway station	o stathmos tu metro (ms)	σταθμός του μετρό
taxi	to taxi (ns)	ταξί
taxi stand	i piatsa taxi (fs)	πιάτσα ταξί
temple	o naos (ms)	ναός
to	se	σε
tourist information	touristekes plirofories	τουριστικέσ πλιροφοριές
tourist office	to grafio turismu (ns)	γραφείο τουρισμού
tower	o pirgos (ms)	πύργος
traffic light	to fanari (ns)	φανάρι
here	etho	εδώ
there	eki	εκεί
far	makria	μακριά
near	konda	κοντά
quite	arteka	αρτεκά
map	o hartis (ms)	χάρτις
next to	thipla sto	δίπλα στο
inside	mesa	πέσα
outside	exo	έξω
over there	eki pera	εκεί πέρα
left	aristera	αριστερά
right	thexia	δεξιά
to the left	pros ta thexia	προς τα δεξιά
to the right	pros ta aristera	προς τα αριστερά
in front of, facing, opposite	brosta	μπροστά
straight	evthia	ευθεία
straight ahead	isia	ίσια
north	voria	βόρεια
south	notia	νότεια
east	anatolika	ανατολικά

west	thitika	δυτικά
zoo	o zoologikos kipos (ms)	ξωολογικός κήποσ

Now let's put them together into some useful sentences to get directions:

I'm lost.	hathika	Χάθηκα
Where is … street?	pu ine othos …	Που είναι οδός …;
How do I get to …?	pos pane se …	Πώς πάνε σε …;
Do you know where the hotel is?	kserete pu ine to'ksenodohio	Ξέρετε πού είναι το ξενοδοχείο;
How far is it?	poso makria ine avto	Πόσο μακριά είναι αυτό;
It's not far.	then ine makria	Δεν είναι μακριά.
Is it near here?	ine etho konda	Είναι εδώ κοντά;
It's near.	ine konda	Είναι κοντά.
It's a bit far.	ine ligho makria	Είναι λίγο μακριά.
It's there.	ine eki	Είναι εκεί.
It's here.	ine etho	Είναι εδώ.
The museum is there.	to musio ine eki	το μουσείο είναι εκεί.
Where are you going?	pu pate	Πού πάτε;
Thanks a lot.	efharisto poli	Ευχαριστώ πολύ.
It's (not) allowed.	(then) epitrepete	(δεν) επιτρέπετε.
Where is the museum on the map?	pu ine to musio ston hartis	Που είναι το μουσείο στον χάρτης;
It's on the right.	ine sta thexia	Είναι στα δεξιά.
Turn left at … street.	stripste aristera stin othos …	Στρίψτε αριστερά στην οδός …
Turn left at the corner and then right.	stripste aristera sti gonia ke meta thexia	Στρίψτε αριστερά στη γωνία και μετά δεξιά.
At the first traffic light.	sto proto fanari	Στο πρώτο φανάρι.
Yes, there is.	ne iparhi	Ναι υπάρχει.

No, there isn't.	ohi then iparhi	Όχι, δεν υπάρχει.
Go straight ahead.	piyene evthia brosta	Πηγαίνε ευθεία μπροστά.
At the end.	sto telos	Στο τέλος.
Turn right at the traffic light.	stripste thexia sto fanari	Στρίψτε δεξιά στο φανάρι.
Behind the church.	piso apo tin eklisia	Πίσω από την εκκλησία.
Where is the bus stop?	pu ine i stasi leoforiu	Που είναι η στάσι λεωφορείο;
Take bus number 8.	parte to leoforio numero octo	Πάρτε το λεωφορείο νούμερο οκτώ.
This is bus number 6.	avto ine to leoforio numero exi	Αυτό είναι το λεωφορείο νούμερο έξι.
Where is the taxi station?	pu ine i piatsa taxi	Που είναι η πιάτσα ταξί;
There is no pharmacy here.	then iparhi farmakio etho	Δεν υπάρχει φαρμακείο εδώ.
I want to go to the hotel.	thelo na pao sto'ksenodohio	Θέλω να πάο στο ξενοδοχείο.
I am staying the hotel.	meno sto'ksenodohio	Μένω στο ξενοδοχείο.
In the center of town.	kendro tis polis	κέντρο της πόλης.
Is it open or closed?	ine avikti I klisti	είναι ανοικτί ή κλειστή
Closed until three.	klista mehri tris	Κλειστά μέχρι τρεις.

Verbs - Past Tense (G)

Now it's time for some grammar. We are going to deal with the past tense. In Greek the past tense is handled by adding suffixes to the verb root. Here is the list of suffixes used to conjugate the past tense of a verb:

Voice	Active	Passive
I	-a	-ika
you	-es	-ikes
he/she/it	-es	-ike
we	-ame	-ikame
you	-ate	-ikate
they	-an	-an

This is the regular past tense conjugation of the active verb 'I said':

I said	ipa	είπα
You said	ipes	είπες
He/she/it said	ipe	είπε
We said	ipame	είπαμε
You said	ipate	είπατε
They said	ipan	είπαν

Here is the regular past tense conjugation for the active verb 'I go':

I went	piga	πήγα
You went	piyes	πήγες
He/she/it went	piye	πήγε
We went	pigame	πήγαμε
You went	pigate	πήγατε
They went	pigan	πήγαν

This is the regular past tense conjugation of the passive verb 'I thought':

I thought	skeptika	σκέφτηκα
You thought	skeptikes	σκέφτηκες
He/she/it thought	skeptike	σκέφτηκε
We thought	skeptikame	σκεφτήκαμε
You thought	skeptikate	σκεφτήκατε
They thought	skeptikan	σκέφτηκαν

However there are also verbs with irregular past tense conjugation. Here is the past tense conjugation for the verb 'I am':

I was	imun	ήμουν
You were	isun	ήσουν
He/she/it was	itan	ήταν
We were	imastan	ήμασταν
You were	isastan	ήσασταν
They were	itan	ήταν

Past Tense Verbs

Here is the first person singular ('I' form) for various verbs:

I arrived	eftasa	έφτασα
I asked	rotisa	ρώτησα
I ate	efaga	έφαγα
I bought	agorasa	αγόρασα
I broke	espasa	έσπασα
I called	kalesa	κάλεσα
I came	irtha	ήρθα
I could, was able	borusa	μπορούσα
I drove	othigisa	οδήγησα
I forgot	ksehasa	ξέχασα
I found	vrika	βρήκα
I gave	ethosa	έδωσα
I got	pira	πήρα
I had	iha	είχα
I knew	ixera	ήξερα
I phoned	tilifonisa	τηλεφώνησα
I lost	ehasa	έχασα
I made, did	ekana	έκανα
I met	gnorisa	γνώρισα
I missed	ehasa	έχασα
I sold	poulisa	πούλησα
I sat	kathisa	κάθισα

I saw	itha	έιδα
I said	ipa	είπα
I spent	perasa	πέρασα
I spoke	milisa	μίλησα
I stayed	emina	έμεινα
I stood	stathika	στάθηκα
I swam	kolibisa	κολύμπησα
I thought	nomisa	νόμισα
I took	pira	πήρα
I understood	katalava	κατάλαβα
I walked	perpatisa	περπάτησα
I wanted	ithela	ήθελα
I was	imun	ήμουν
I went	piga	πήγα

Here are some examples:

I ate an orange.	efaga ena portokali	Έφαγα ένα πορτοκάλι
I arrived yesterday.	eftasa hthes	Έφτασα χθες
I wanted a taxi.	ithela ina taxi	Ήθελα ένα ταξί
I wanted to go the bank.	ithela na pao stin trapeza	Ήθελα να πάω στην τράπεζα
I bought a book.	agorasa ena vivlio	Αγόρασα ένα βιβλίο.
I lost my wallet.	ehasa to portofoli mu	Έχασα το πορτοφόλι μου.
I missed the train.	ehasa to treno	Έχασα το τρένο.
When did you phone?	pote tha tilefoniso	Πότε θα τηλεφωνήσω;
I phoned in the evening.	tilifonisa to vrathi	Τηλεφώνησα το βράδυ.
I stayed at Patras.	emina stin patra	Έμεινα στην Πάτρα.
I gave you 10 euros.	sas ethosa theka evro	Σας έδωσα δέκα ευρώ.

Notice that in the past tense in Greek you don't need to use the first or second person pronouns 'I' or 'you' because they are understood from the ending of the verb.

Verbs - Future Tense (G)

Now it's time for some more grammar. We are going to deal with the future tense. In Greek the future tense is formed by using the word **tha** (equivalent of 'will' in English) and the present tense verb. In some cases the verb does not change, but usually the verb does change.

The following verbs do not change in the future tense.

I will be	tha ime	θα είμαι
I will do	tha kano	θα κάνω
I will have	tha eho	θα έχω
I will know	tha ksero	θα ξέρω
I will go	tha pao	θα πάω

Here is the future tense conjugation for the verb 'I do':

I will do	tha kano	Θα κάνω
You will do	tha kanis	Θα κάνεις
He/she/it will do	tha kanes	Θα κάνες
We will do	tha kanume	Θα κάνουμε
You will do	tha kanete	Θα κάνετε
They will do	tha kanoun	Θα κάνουν

The following verbs do change in the future tense.

I will bring	tha fero	θα φέρω
I will give	tha thoso	θα δώσω
I will leave	tha afiso	θα αφήσω
I will send	tha stilo	θα στείλω
I will stay	tha mino	θα μείνω

I will take	tha paro	θα πάρω
I will want	tha theliso	θα θελήσω
I will write	tha grapso	θα γράψω

Here is the complete future tense conjugation for the verb 'I write':

I will write	tha grapso	θα γράψω
You will write	tha grapsis	θα γράψεις
He/she/it will write	tha grapsi	θα γράψει
We will write	tha grapsume	θα γράψουμε
You will write	tha grapso	θα γράψω
They will write	tha grapsun	θα γράψουν

This table shows the conjugation of the verb 'I would like' which we encountered before in the chapter on Expressing Wants and Needs.

I would like	tha ithela	Θα ήθελα
You would like	tha itheles	Θα ήθελες
He/she/it would like	tha ithele	Θα ήθελε
We would like	tha thelame	Θα θέλαμε
You would like	tha thelate	Θα θέλατε
They would like	tha ithelan	Θα ήθελαν

These words are typically contracted, for example, tha ithela is typically said as tha'thela. These are often used with the word na to connect to a second verb to express 'I would like to ...'.

| I would like to eat something. | tha ithela na fao kati | Θα ήθελα να φάω κάτι. |
| He would like to eat at 9 o'clock. | tha ithele na fai stis enia | Θα ήθελε να φάει στις εννιά. |

The na connector word is also used where two verbs in the same sentence have different pronouns.

53

I want us to go.	thelo na pame	Θέλω να πάμε.
He wants me to go.	theli na pao	Θέλει να πάω.
They want him to go.	thelun na pai	Θέλουν να πάει.

Here are some more examples of the future tense:

We will eat at 9 o'clock.	tha fame stis enia	Θα φάμε στις εννιά.
He would like to eat at 9 o'clock.	tha ithele na fai stis enia	Θα ήθελε να φάει στις εννιά.
He will come in the morning.	tha erthi to proi	Θα έρθει το πρωί.
I will give you 5 dollars.	tha sas doso pende dolaria	Θα σας δώσω πέντε δολάρια.
We will stay one week.	tha minume mia evthomatha	Θα μείνουμε μία εβδομάδα.

At the Restaurant

There are several different types of eating establishments you will encounter in Greece:

delicatessen	alandika	ΑΛΑΝΤΙΚΑ
coffee shop	kafenio	ΚΑΦΕΝΕΊΟ
fish restaurant	psarotaverna	ΨΑΡΟΤΑΒΕΡΝΑ
grilled meat taverna	psistaria	ΨΗΣΤΑΡΙΑ
kebab shop	suvlatzithiko	ΣΟΥΛΑΚΙ
restaurant	estiatorio	ΕΣΤΑΤΟΡΙΟ
pastry shop	zaharoplastio	ΖΑΧΑΡΟΠΛΑΣΤΕΙΟ

Let's go to the restaurant estiatorio and order some delicious Greek food fayito. Getting started:

| appetizer, | to orektiko (ns) | ΟΡΕΚΤΙΚΟ |

starter		
breakfast	to proino (ns)	πρωινό
lunch	mesimeriano	μεσημεριανό
dinner	vrathino	βραδινό
dish, course	piato	πιάτο
dessert	gliko	γλυκό
Bon appétit	kali orexi	Καλή όρεξη
chair	i karekla (fs)	καρέκλα
cup	to kupa (ns)	κούπα
eat (v)	troo	τρώω
food	to fayito (ns)	Φαγητό
fork	to piruni (ns)	Πιρούνι
bill, check	to logariasmo (ns)	λογαριασμό
glass	to potiri (ns)	ποτήρι
plate	to piato (ns)	πιάτο
knife	to maheri (ns)	μαχαίρι
a little, some	ligo (ms), ligi (fs), ligo (ns)	λίγο
a lot	poli	πολύ
menu	menu	μενού
napkin	petseta	πετσέτα
meal	to yevma (ns)	γεύμα
snack	prohiro fagito	πρόχειρο φαγητό
service	exipiretisi	εξυπηρέτηση
signature	i ipografo (fs)	υπογράφω
special	ithikos	ειδικός
spoon	to kutali (ns)	κουτάλι
table	to trapeza (ns)	τραπέζι
taste	i yevsi (fs)	γεύση
savor, taste	yevome (v)	γεύομαι
spicy	pikantikos	πικάντικος
sour	ksini	ξινή
toothpick	i othontoglifida (fs)	οδοντογλυφίδα
vegetarian	i hortofagos (fs)	χορτοφάγος
waiter	o servitoros (ms)	σερβιτόρος
waitress	i servitora (fs)	σερβιτόρα

Let's start with breakfast proino:

bread	to psomi (ns)	ψωμί
butter	to vutiro (ns)	βούτιρο
cereal	to thimitriaka (ns)	δημητριακά
egg	to avgo (ns)	αυγό
hard-boiled egg	to skliro vrasto avgo (ns)	σκληρό βραστό αυγό
honey	to meli (ns)	μέλι
salt	to alati (ns)	αλάτι
pepper	to piperi (ns)	πιπέρι
slice	i feta (ns)	φέτα
toast	frigania	φρυγανιά

Now for lunch mesimeriano:

beef	moshari	μοσχάρι
cheese pie	i tiropita (fs)	τυόπιττα
fish	to psari (ns)	ψάρι
fries	i patates (fp)	πατάτες
fried	tiganitos	τηγανιτός
boiled	vrasmenos	βρασμένος
grilled	psitos	ψιτός
cabbage	to lahano (ns)	λάχανο
carrots	ta karota (np)	καρότα
cheese	to tiri (ns)	τυρί
chicken	to kotopulo (ns)	κοτόπουλο
chick peas	ta revithia (ns)	ρεβύθια
corn	to kalaboki (ns)	καλαμπόκι
cucumber	to aguri (ns)	αγγούρι
eggplant	i melitzana (fs)	μελιτζάνα
garlic	to skortho (ns)	σκόρδο
jelly, jam	ores	ώρες
kebab	to kebap (ns)	κεμπάπ
lamb	to arni (ns)	αρνί
lamb chop	to arni brizola (ns)	αρνί μπριζόλα
lettuce	to maruli (ns)	μαρούλι
fresh	freskos	φρέσκος
meat	to kreas (ns)	κρέας
mushroom	to manitari (ns)	μανιτάρι

olives	i elies (fp)	ελιές
olive oil	to eleolatha (ns)	ελαιόλαδο
onion	to kremithi (ns)	κρεμμύδι
pea	arakas	αρακάς
pork	to hirino (ns)	χοιρινό
pork chop	to hirino brizola (ns)	χοιρινό μπριζόλα
potato	i patata (fs)	πατάτα
prawns	garithes (np)	γαρίδες
rice	to rizi (ns)	ρύζι
salad	i salata (fs)	σαλάτα
sauce	i saltsa (fs)	Σάλτσα
sausage	to lukaniko (ns)	Λουκάνικο
savory	almiro	αλυμιρό
seafood	ta thalasina (np)	Θαλασσινά
tomato	i domata (fs)	ντοματα
soup	i supa (fs)	σούπα
spaghetti	ta makaronia (np)	μακαρόνια
spicy	pikandikos	πικάντικος
spinach	to spanaki (ns)	σπανάκι
squid	kalamaria	καλαμάρια
steak	i brizola (fs)	μπριζόλα
sugar	i zahari (fs)	ζάχαρη
vegetable	to lahaniko (ns)	λαχανικό
vinegar	to ksithi (ns)	ξύδι

Greek specialities:

cheesepie	tiropita	τυρόπιτα
meatpie	kreatopita	κρεατπιτα
meatballs	keftethes	κεφτέδες
saganaki (fried cheese)	saganaki	σαγανάκι
spanakopita (spinach pie)	spanakopita	σπανακόπιτα
souvlaki (grilled lamb in a pita)	suvlaki	σουλάκι
kalamaki (lamb kebab)	kalamaki	καλαμάκι

mousaka	musa<u>ka</u>s	μουσακάς
sesame ring	ku<u>lu</u>ri	κουλούρι
taramosalata (fish-roe dip)	taramosa<u>la</u>ta	ταραμοσαλάτα
tzatziki (yoghurt & garlic dip)	tzat<u>zi</u>ki	τζατζίκι

Now for the drinks:

coffee	o ka<u>fe</u> (ms)	καφέ
medium	<u>me</u>trio	μέτριο
sweet	gli<u>ko</u>	γλυκό
without sugar	s<u>ke</u>to	σκέτο
black coffee	o ka<u>fe</u> (ms)	καφέ
iced coffee	fra<u>pe</u>	φραπέ
bottle	to bu<u>ka</u>li (ns)	μπουκάλι
bottle opener	to anah<u>ti</u>ri (ns)	ανοιχτήρι
half bottle	to mik<u>ro</u> bu<u>ka</u>li (ns)	μικρό μπουκάλι
beer	i <u>bi</u>ra (fs)	μπύρα
can (soda)	to ku<u>ti</u> (ns)	κουτί
corkscrew	to anah<u>ti</u>ri (ns)	ανοιχτήρι
milk	to <u>ga</u>la (ns)	γάλα
drink (v)	<u>pi</u>no	πίνω
ice	o <u>pa</u>gos (ms)	πάγος
juice	o hi<u>mos</u> (ms)	χυπός
apple juice	o <u>mi</u>lu hi<u>mo</u> (fs)	μήλου χυπό
lemonade	i lemo<u>na</u>tha (fs)	λεμονάδα
orange juice	o porto<u>ka</u>li hi<u>mo</u> (ms)	πορτοκάλι χυπό
tea	to tse (ns)	τσάι
tea bag	to fake<u>la</u>ki tse (ns)	φακελάκι τσάι
teapot	i tsayi<u>e</u>ra (fs)	τσαγιέρα
tea with milk	to tse me <u>ga</u>la (ns)	τσάι με γάλα
tea with lemon	to tse me le<u>mo</u>ni (ns)	τσάι με λεμόνι
wine	to kra<u>si</u> (ns)	κρασί
red wine	to <u>ko</u>kinos kra<u>si</u> (ns)	κόκκινος κρασί
white wine	to <u>a</u>spro kra<u>si</u> (ns)	άσπρο κρασί
soda	i <u>so</u>tha (fs)	σόδα
water	to ne<u>ro</u> (ns)	νερό

glass of water	to potiri nero (ns)	ποτήρι νερό

Let's finish with a dessert epidorpio. Greeks love fruit fruto for dessert:

dessert	to epidorpio (ns)	επιδόρπιο
dessert	gliko	γλυκό
apple	to milo (ns)	μήλο
apple pie	i milopita (fs)	μηλόπιτα
apricot	to verikoko (ns)	βερίκοκο
banana	i banana (fs)	μπανάνα
cake	to kake (ns)	κέικ
cookie	to biskoto (ns)	μπισκότο
cherry	to kerasi (ns)	κεράσι
chocolate	i sokolata (fs)	σοκολάτα
fruit	fruto	φρούτο
fig	to siko (ns)	σύκο
grape	to stafili (ns)	σταφύλι
grapefruit	to grapefruit (ns)	γκρέιπ φρουτ
icecream	to pagoto (ns)	παγωτό
melon	to meloni (ns)	πεπόνι
orange	to portokali (ns)	πορτοκάλι
peach	to rothakino (ns)	ροδάκινο
pear	to ahladi (ns)	αχλάδι
plum	to thamaskino (ns)	δαμάσκηνο
pineapple	o ananas (ms)	ανανάς
raspberry	to vatomuro (ns)	βατόμουρο
strawberry	i fraula (fs)	φράουλα
sweet	glikos	γλυκός
sour	ksini	ξινή
tangerine	to mandarini (ns)	μανταρίνι
watermelon	to karpuzi (ns)	καρπούζι

Phrases:

Do you serve food?	servirete fayito	Σερβίρετε φαγητό;
I have booked a	ego klisi trapezi ya	Εγώ κλείσει

table for two.	thio	τραπέζι για δύο.
A table for two please.	ena trapezi ya thio parakalo	Ένα τραπέζι για δύο παρακαλώ.
We want to have breakfast.	thelume na ehume proino	Θέλουμε να έχουμε πρωινό
Do you have ...?	ehete...	Έχετε ...;
The menu please.	to menu parakalo	το μενού παρακαλώ.
I would like ...	tha ithela ...	Θα ήθελα ...
I want ...	thelo ...	Θέλω ...
I want to pay.	thelo na pliroso	Θέλω να πληρώσω.
A glass of milk please.	ena potiri gala parakalo	Ένα ποτήρι γάλα παρακαλώ.
I want to drink some wine.	thelo na pio ligo krasi	Θέλω να πιω λίγο κρασί.
I would like to eat mousaka.	tha ithela na fao musaka	Θα ήθελα να φάω μουσακά.
I want to order.	thelo na paragilo	Θέλω να παραγγείλω.
Is service included?	ine me to servis	Είναι με το σερβίς;
I'm hungry.	ime pinasmenos	Είμαι πεινασμένος
What would you like to drink?	ti tha thelete na pite	Τι θα θέλετε να πιείτε;
What would you like to eat?	ti tha thelete na fate	Τι θα θέλετε να φάτε;
Do you have fresh fish?	ehete freska-psaria	Έχετε φρέσκα ψάρια;
What do you recommend?	ti protinete	Τι προτείνετε;
Bring me ...	ferte mu ...	Φέρτε μου ...
Give me ...	those mu ...	Δώσε μου ...
What is this?	ti ine avto	τι είναι αυτό;
What is that?	ti ine ekino	Τι είναι εκείνο;
Do you like it? (Does it please you?)	su aresi	Σου αρέσει;
It's too cold.	ine para poli krio	Είναι πάρα πολύ κρύο.

It's too hot.	ine para poli kavto	Είναι πάρα πολύ καυτό.
That's all.	avta	Αυτά.
A few, any	merika	μερικά
Delicious!	nostimo	Νόστιμο!
The bill please.	to logariasmo parakalo	Το λογαριασμό παρακαλό
That is very good.	avto ine poli kalo	Αυτό έιναι πολύ καλό.
Would you like something to drink?	tha thelete na pite kati	Θα θέλετε να πιείτε κάτι;
What are you drinking?	ti pinis	Τι πίνεις;
What will you drink?	ti tha pite	Τι θα πιείτε;
Would you like to drink wine?	tha thelete na pite krasi	Θα θέλετε να πίνουν κρασί;
What do you want to drink?	ti tha thelete ne pite	Τι θα θέλετε να πιείτε;
I want a glass of red wine.	thelo ena potiri kokino krasi	Θέλω ένα ποτήρι κόκκινο κρασί.
I want a bottle of white wine.	thelo ena bukali levko krasi	Θέλω ένα μπουκάλι λευκό κρασί.
I'm a vegetarian.	ime hortofagos	Είμαι χορτοφάγος
The fish is very tasty.	to psari ine poli nostimo	Το ψάρι είναι πολύ νόστιμο.
Do you like ice-cream?	sas arese to pagoto	Σας άρεσε το παγωτό;
Ok. It's ok.	endaxi	Εντάξει.
Bon appétit!	kali orexi	Καλή όρεξη!
I'm drinking retsina.	pino retsina	Πίνω ρετσίνα.
Give me a bite.	those mu mia bukia	Δώσε μου μια μπουκιά.
Give me a sip.	those mu mia gulia	Δώσε μου μια γουλιά.

Chatting at the table.

Excellent.	exeretiko	Εξαιρετικό!
Cheers	stin iya mas	Στην υγειά μας.
Good, thanks!	kala efharisto	Καλά ευχαριστώ
Very good.	poli kala	Πολύ καλά.
Of course	veveos	βεβαίως.
Good luck	kali tihi	Καλή τύχη.
Excuse me.	signomi	Συγγνώμη.
I'm sorry.	lipame	Λυπάμαι.
Really?	alithia	Αλήθεια;
Certainly!	sigura	Σίγουρα!
What do you like to do?	ti sas aresi na kanete	Τι σας αρέσει να κάνετε;
I like to travel.	mu aresi na taxithevo	Μου αρέσει να ταξίδεύω.
Do you have children?	ehete pethia	Έχετε παιδιά;
I have three children.	eho tria pethia	Έχω τρία παιδιά.
We have a boy and a girl.	ehume en'agori ke ena koritsi	Έχουμε ένα αγόρι και ένα κορίτσι.
How old are they?	poso hronon ine	Πόσο χρονών είναι;
It's not necessary.	then ine aparetito	Δεν είναι απαραίτητο.
It doesn't matter.	then pirazi	Δεν πειράζει.
What do you want to do?	ti thelete na kanete	Τι θέλετε να κάνετε;
Bye, talk to you later.	ya ta lene	Γεια τα λένε.
One moment.	mia stigmi	Πια στιγμή.
Let's go.	pame	Πάμε.

Pronouns (G)

Subject Pronouns

Here are the personal pronouns as the subject (nominative) of a sentence. These pronouns are rarely used in Greek because the subject to whom the verb is referring is obvious from the verb ending itself. Typically they are only used for emphasis.

I	**ego**	εγώ
you	**esi**	εσύ
he	**avtos** (ms)	αυτός
she	**avti** (fs)	αυτή
it	**avto** (ns)	αυτό
we	**emis**	εμείς
you	**esis**	εσείς
they	**avti** (mp)	αυτοί
they	**avtes** (fp)	αυτές
they	**avta** (np)	αυτά

Direct Object Pronouns

Here are the personal pronouns as the direct object (accusative) of a sentence.

me	me	με
you	se	σε
him	ton (ms)	τον
her	tin (fs)	την
it	to (ns)	το
us	mas	μας

you	sas	σας
them	tus (mp)	τους
them	tis (fp)	τις
them	ta (np)	τα

These are placed before the verb. Here are some examples:

Do you understand me?	me katalavenis	Με καταλαβαίνεις;
I see her.	tin vlepo	Την βλέπω.
I buy it (ms)	ton agorazo	τον αγοράζω
I buy it (ns)	to agorazo	το αγοράζω
I buy them (np)	ta agorazo	τα αγοράζω
He has them.	tis ehi	Τις έχει.
We have them.	ta ehume	Τα έχουμε.
I can help you.	boro na sas voithiso	Μπορώ να σας βοηθήσω.

Indirect Object Pronouns

Here are the personal pronouns as the indirect object of a sentence with the preposition 'to', 'towards' or 'at'. The indirect object pronoun is placed before the verb.

me	mu	μου
you	su	σου
him, it	tu	του
her	tis	της
us	mas	μας
you	sas	σας
them	tus	τους

Here are some examples in the present tense:

I speak to him.	tu milao	Του μιλάω.
I give the wine to her.	tis thino to krasi	Της δίνω το κρασί

Possessive Pronouns (G)

To show ownership of something in Greek, you use the possessive pronoun which goes after the noun.

my	mu	μου
your	su	σου
his / its	tu	του
her	tis	της
our	mas	μας
your	sas	σας
their	tus	τους

Here are some examples of their usage. Notice that the noun also has its preceding article:

My handbag	i tsanda mu	η τσάντα μου
Is this your handbag?	ine avti i tsanda sas	Είναι αυτή η τσάντα σας;
Your car	to avtokinito su	το αυτοκίνητο σου
Where is my suitcase?	pu ine i valitsa mu	Που είναι η βαλίτσα μου;
Here is your book.	etho ine to vivlio sas	Εδώ είναι το βιβλίο σας.
This is their house.	avto ine to spiti tus	Αυτό είναι το σπίτι τους.
Come to my house.	elate sto spiti mu	Έλάτε στο σπίτι μου.
Our house is very big.	spiti sas ine poli megali	Σπίτι μας είναι πολύ μεγάλη.
My daughter lives in Corinth.	i kori mu meni stin korintho	Η κόρη μου μένει στην Κόρινθο.
My husband is in Patras.	o anthras mu ine stin patra	Ο άνδρας μου είναι στην Πάτρα.

Demonstrative Pronouns

this	avtos (ms) avti (fs) avto (ns)	αυτός αυτή αυτό
these	avti (mp) avtes (fp) avta (np)	αυτοί αυτές αυτά
that	ekinos (ms) ekini (fs) ekino (ns)	εκείνος εκείνη εκείνο
those	ekini (mp) ekines (fp) ekina (np)	εκείνοι εκείνες εκείνα

Family

If you are visiting family ikoyenia these words will be useful:

anniversary	i epetios (fs)	επέτειος
apartment	to thiamerisma (ns)	διαμέρισμα
birthday	to genethlia (ns)	γενέθλια
celebration	o eortasmos (ms)	εορτασμός
married	pandremenos	παντρεμένος
wedding, marriage	o gamos (ms)	γάμος
bride	i nifi (fs)	νύφη
bridegroom	o gambros (ms)	γαμπρός
single	elevtheros (ms)	ελεύθερος
single	elevtheri (fs)	ελεύθερη
Happy Birthday	hronia pola	Χρόνια πολλά
Thanksgiving	efharisties	Ευχαριστίες
photograph	i fotografia (fs)	φωτογραφία
hug	i angalia (fs)	αλκαλιά
residence	i katikia (fs)	κατοικία

visit (v)	episkeptome	επισκέπτομαι
visit	i episkepsi (fs)	επίσκεψη
mother	i mitera (fs)	μητέρα
father	o pateras (ms)	πατέρας
parents	i gonis (fs)	γονείς
baby	to moro (ns)	μωρό
wife	i yineka (fs)	γυναίκα
sister	i athelfi (fs)	αδελφή
brother	o athelfos (ms)	αδελφός
daughter	i kori (fs)	κόρη
son	o yios (ms)	γιός
nephew	o anipsios (ms)	ανιψιός
niece	i anipsia (fs)	ανιψιά
cousin	o ksatherfos (ms)	ξάδερφος
cousin	i ksatherfi (fs)	ξαδέρφη
uncle	o thios (ms)	θείος
aunt	i thia (fs)	θεία
grandmother	i yaya (fs)	γιαγιά
grandfather	o papus (ms)	παππούς
granddaughter	i engoni (fs)	εγγονή
grandson	o engonos (ms)	εγγονός
father-in-law	o petheros (ms)	πεθερός
mother-in-law	i pethera (fs)	Πεθερά

Phrases:

How is your family?	pos ine i ikoyenia sas	Πώς είναι η οικογένεια σας;
How is your daughter?	pos ine i kori sas	Πώς είναι η κόρη σας;
This is my husband.	apo tho o anthras mu	Από 'δω ο άνδρας μου.
This is my wife.	apo tho i yineka mu	Από 'δω η γυναίκα μου.
This is my spouse.	apo tho o sizigos mu	Από 'δω ο σύζυγός μου.
This is my good (male) friend.	apo tho o kalos filos mu	Από 'δω ο καλός φίλος μου.
This is my	apo tho i fili mu	Από 'δω η φίλη

(female) friend.		μου.
I have a son.	eho ena yio	Έχω ένα γιο.
How old are you?	poson hronon ise	Πόσον χρονών είσαι;
I am ... years old.	ime ... hronon	Είμαι ... χρονών.
Are you married?	iste pantemenos	Είστε παντρεμένος;
My son is very well.	o yios mu ine poli kala	Ο γιος μου είναι πολύ καλά.
Happy birthday.	hronia pola	Χρονιά πολλά
Happy New Year	kali hronia	Καλή χρονιά.
Happy Christmas.	kala hristuyena	Καλά χριστούγεννα.
For me.	ya mena	Για μένα.
It's for you.	ine ya sas	Είναι για σας.

Traveling

Look out for these signs:

Arrivals	afixis	ΑΦΙΞΕΙΣ
Customs	telonion	ΤΕΛΩΝΕΙΟΝ
Departures	anahorisis	ΑΝΑΧΩΡΗΣΕΙΣ
Platform	platforma	ΠΛΑΤΦΟΡΜΑ
Ticket Office	grafio isitirion	ΓΡΑΦΕΙΟ ΕΙΣΙΤΗΡΙΩΝ
Left Luggage	thirithes aposkegon	ΘΥΡΙΔΕΣ ΑΠΟΣΚΕΥΩΝ
Bus Stop	stasi	ΣΤΑΣΙ

Here are some useful words for travelling:

arrive (v)	ftano	φθάνω
arrival	i afixi (fs)	άφιξη
airplane	to eroplano (ns)	αεροπλάνο
airport	to erothromio (ns)	αεροδρόμιο
application	i etisi (fs)	αίτηση

baggage	i aposkeves (fp)	αποσκευές
country	i hora (fs)	χώρα
delayed	kathisterisi	καθυστέρηση
departure	i anahorisi (fs)	αναχώρηση
driver	o othigos (ms)	οδηγός
travel (v)	taxithevo	ταξίδεύω
first class seat	i proti thesi (fs)	πρώτη θέση
second class seat	i thefteri thesi (fs)	δεύτερη θέση
flight	i ptisi (fs)	πτήση
fly (v)	petao	πετάω
hotel	to ksenodohio (ns)	ξενοδοχείο
on time	stin ora	στην ώρα
passport	to thiavatirio (ns)	διαβατήριο
rent, hire (v)	nikiazo	νικιάζω
schedule	to programma (ns)	Πρόγραμμα
suitcase	i valitsa (fs)	Βαλίτσα
land (v)	prosyionete	προσγειώνεται
platform	i platorma (fs)	πλατφόρμα
seat	i thesi (fs)	θέση
take off (v)	apoyionete	απογειώνεται
taxi	to taxi (ns)	ταξί
ticket	to isitirio (ns)	Εισιτήριο
roundtrip ticket	isitirio me epistrofis	εισιτήριο με επιστροφής
ticket office	to grafio isitirion (ns)	Γραφείο εισιτηρίων
timetable	to hrono-thiagrama (ns)	χρονο διάγραμμα
tour	i periothia (fs)	Περιοδεία
train	to treno (ns)	Τρένο
train station	o stathmos trenon (ms)	σταθμός τρένων
travel agency	to taxithiotiko grafio (ns)	ταξίδιωτικό γραφείο
traveler	o taxithiotis (ms)	ταξιδιώτις
vacation , holiday	i thiakopes (fp)	διακοπές
visa	i visa (fs)	βίζα

Here are some more words to help you get money lefta when you arrive.

teller	to tamias trapezas (ns)	ταμίας τράπεζας
cash machine (ATM)	to mihani analipsis (ns)	μηχάνι ανάληψης
bank	i trapeza (fs)	τράπεζα
credit	i pistosi (fs)	πίστωση
credit card	i pistotiki karta(fs)	πιστωτική κάρτα
change	i alaxo (fs)	αλλάξω
coins	ta kermata (np)	κέρματα
exchange (v)	anatalaxo	ανταλλάξω
money	ta lefta (np)	λεφτά
traveler's check	taxithiotikes epitayes	ταξίδιωτικές επιταγές

When you travel you may want to know these useful phrases:

Bon voyage.	kalo taxithi	Καλό ταξίδι.
Have a nice stay.	kali thiamoni	Καλή διαμονή.
Where can I buy a ticket?	pu boro n'agoraso ena isitirio	Πού μπορώ να αγοράσω ένα εισιτήριο;
I want a ticket to Patras.	thelo ena isitirio stin patra	Θέλω ένα εισιτήριο στην Πάτρα.
We are going to Corfu (Kerkira).	pame stin kerkira	Πάμε στην Κέρκυρα.
I am from ...	ime apo to ...	Είμαι απώ το ...
How much is a ticket to Corinth?	poso ine ena isitirio ya tin korintho	Πόσο είναι ένα εισιτήριο για την Κόρινθο;
Where is the bus to Corinth?	pu ine to leoforio ya korintho	που είναι το λεωφορείο για Κόρινθο;
Passport and ticket please.	thiavatirio ke to isitirio parakalo	Διαβατήριο και το εισιτήριο παρακαλώ.
We don't have tickets.	then ehume isitiria	Δεν έχουμε εισιτήρια.

I want to book a seat.	thelo na klisete mia thesi	Θέλω να κλείσετε μια θέση.
Here is my passport.	etho ine to thiavatirio mu	Εδώ είναι το διαβατήριό μου.
Where are you from? (formal)	apo pu iste	Από πού είστε;
Where are you from? (informal)	apo pu ise	Από πού είσαι;
I am on vacation.	ime se thiakopes	Είμαι σε διακοπές.
I will fly on Monday.	tha petaxi tin theftera	Θα πετάξει την Δευτέρα.
Where do I take ...?	apo pu perno ...	Από που παίρνω ...
How long have you been here?	poso kero ehete etho	Πόσο καιρό έχετε εδώ.
When did you arrive?	pote tha ftasete	Πότε θα φτάσετε;
Where is the currency exchange?	pu ine to grafio sinalagmatos	Πού είναι το γραφείο συναλλάγματος;
Where can I rent a car?	pu boro na nikiaso avtokinito	Πού μπορώ να νοικιάσω ένα αυτοκίνητο;
Where can I rent a cellphone?	pu boro na nikiaso ena kinito tilefono	Πού μπορώ να νοικιάσω ένα κινητό τηλέφωνο;
Where is a cash machine (ATM)?	pu ine to avtomato mihanika analipsis	Πού είναι το αυτόματο μηχάνικα ανάληψης;
Where is the bank?	pu ine i trapeza	Πού είναι η τράπεζα;
Is there a bank near here?	iparhi trapeza etho konda	Υπάρχει τράπεζα εδώ κοντά;
Do you take credit cards?	pernete pistotikes kartes	Παίρετε πιστοτικές κάρτες;
I want to change money.	thelo na alaxo lefta	Θέλω να αλλάξω λεφτά.
In dollars.	se dolaria	Σε δολάρια
Do you have any	ehete merika evro	Έχετε μερικά

euros?		ευρώ.
How many euros do you have?	posa evro ehete	Πόσα ευρώ έχετε;
I want to exchange money.	thelo na antalaxo lefta	Θέλω να ανταλλάξω λεφτά.
I want to exchange dollars for euros.	thelo na antalaxo dolaria ya evro	Θέλω να ανταλλάξω δολάρια για ευρώ.
Sign here.	engrafite etho	Εγγραφείτε εδώ.

Prepositions (G)

Here are Greek prepositions. Commonly used prepositions include: se meaning 'at, in, to'; me meaning 'with, by'; apo meaning 'from, of'; and ya meaning 'for'.

above	pano apo	πάνω από
after	meta	μετά
against	kata	κατά
among	anamesa	ανάμεσα
around	yiro	γύρω
at, in, to	se	σε
before, in front of	brosta	μπροστά
between	metaxi	μεταξύ
below, under	ipo	υπό
beside	thipla	δίπλα
for	ya	για
from, of	apo	από
inside	mesa se	πέσα σε
near, close to	konda se	κοντά σε
on	pano se	πάνω σε
outside	exo	έξω
over (above)	epano	επάνω
towards	pros	προς
under	kato apo	κάτω από
until	mehri	μέχρι
with , by	me	με

without	horis	χορίς

Often prepositions and combined with an article. Here are some common contractions:

se + ton	ston (ms)	στον
se + tin	stin (fs)	στην
se + to	sto (ns)	στο
se + tus	stus (mp)	στους
se + tis	stis (fp)	στης
se + ta	sta (np)	στα

Here are some examples:

on the map	ston hartis	στον χάρτης
in/to the city	stin polis	στην πόλη
to the hotel	sto ksenodohio	στο ξενοδοχείο

And now for some examples of their usage:

The book is on the table.	to vivlio ine pano sto trapezi	Το βιβλίο είναι πάνω στο τραπέζι.
I have a hat on my head.	eho ena kapelo sto kefali mu	Έχω ένα καπέλο στο κεφάλι μου.
Around here	etho yiro	εδώ γύρω
The book is under the chair.	to vivlio ine kato apo tin karelka	Το βιβλίο είναι κάτω από την καρέκλα.
I am talking on my cellphone.	milao sto kinito mu	Μιλάω στο κινητό μου.
I drank from the bottle.	epina apo to bukali	Έπινα από το μπουκάλι.
From Patras to Athens.	apo tin patra stin athina	Από την Πάτρα στην Αθήνα.
He is going to the hotel.	piyeni sto'ksenodohio	Πηγαίνει στο ξενοδοχείο.
He lives in the big house.	meni sto megalo spiti	Μένει στο μεγάλο σπίτι.
With milk.	me gala	με γάλα

Shopping

Look for these signs:

butcher shop	kreopolion	ΚΡΕΟΠΩΛΕΙΟΝ
bakery	artopolio	ΑΡΤΟΠΩΛΕΙΟ
bookshop	vivliopolio	ΒΙΒΛΙΟΠΩΛΕΙΟ
fruit	fruta	ΦΡΟΥΤΑ
grocery	pantopolion	ΠΑΝΤΟΠΩΛΕΙΟΝ
pastry shop	zaharoplastio	ΖΑΑΧΑΡΟΠΛΑΣΤΕΙΟ
supermarket	supermarket	ΣΟΥΠΕΡΜΑΡΚΕΤ
take-away	se paketo	ΣΕ ΠΑΚΕΤΟ
vegatables	lahanika	ΛΑΧΑΝΙΚΑ
fish shop	psarathiko	ΨΑΡΑΔΙΚΟ
seafood	thalasina	ΘΑΛΑΣΣΙΝΑ

Let's go shopping.

aisle, row	to thiadromo (ns)	διάδρομο
bakery	to artopolio (ns)	αρτοπωλείο
bank	i trapeza (fs)	τράπεζα
basket	to kalathi (ns)	καλάθι
battery	i bataria (fs)	μπαταρία
bookshop	to vivliopolio (ns)	βιβλιοπωλείο
butcher shop	to kreopolio (ns)	κρεοπωείο
camera	i kamera (fs)	κάμερα
cash	ta metrita (np)	μετρητά
cash register, till	to tamio (ns)	ταμείο
cash only	mono metrita	μόνο μετρητά
cheap	ftinos	φτηνός
clothes store	to ruha katastima (ns)	ρούχα κατάστημα
convenience store	to psilikatzithiko (ns)	ψιλικατζίδικο
cosmetics	ta kalindika (np)	καλλυντικά
department store	to polikatastima (ns)	πολυ κατάστημα

dictionary	to lexiko (ns)	λεξικό
expensive	akriva	ακριβά
free of charge	thorean	δωρεάν
gift	to thoro (ns)	δώρο
laundrette	to katharistirio (ns)	καθαριστήριο
grocery	to pandopolio (ns)	παντοπωλείο
loaf of bread	to karveli (ns)	καρβέλι
manager	o thiefthindis (ms)	διευθυντής
market	i agora (fs)	αγορά
fruit and vegetable market	i laiki agora (fs)	Λαϊκή αγορά
parking	o stathmefsi (ms)	στάθμευση
pharmacy	to farmakio (ns)	φαρμακείο
pottery	i keramiki (fs)	κεραμική
price	i timi (fs)	τιμή
receipt	i paralavi (fs)	παραλαβή
rugs	ta halia (np)	χαλιά
sale, discount	i ekptosi (fs)	έκπτωση
sales assistant	i politria (fs)	πωλήτρια
scissors	to psalithi (ns)	ψαλίδι
selection	pikilia	ποικιλία
shop, store	to katastima (ns)	κατάστημα
supermarket	to super market (ns)	σούπερ μαρκετ
travel agency	to taxithiotiko grafio (ns)	ταξίδιωτικό γραφείο
worry beads	ta komboloyia (np)	κομπολόγια

Clothes:

blouse	i bluza (fs)	μπλούζα
bracelet	to vrahioli (ns)	βραχιόλι
boots	i botes (fp)	μπότες
bra	to sutien (ns)	σουτιέν
changing room	to thokimastirio (ns)	δοκιμαστήριο
clothes	ta ruha (np)	ρούχα
coat	to palto (ns)	παλτό
in cotton	vlamvakeros	βαμβακερός
dress	to forema (ns)	φόρεμα

earrings	ta skularikia (np)	σκουλαρίκια
flip-flops	ta sagionares (np)	σαγιονάρες
gloves	ta ganthia (np)	γάνδια
hat	to kapelo (ns)	καπέλο
jacket	to sakaki (ns)	σακάκι
jewellery	ta kosmimata (np)	κοσμήματα
leather	therma	δέρμα
loose	hima	χύμα
tight	sfihtos	σφιχτός
necklace	to kolie (ns)	κολλιέ
ring	o thaktilios (ms)	δακτύλιος
sandals	ta sandalia (np)	σανδάλια
scarf	to kashkol (ns)	κασκόλ
shirt	to pukamisa (ns)	πουκάμις
shoes	ta paputsia (np)	παπούτσια
shorts	ta sorts (np)	σορτς
size	to meyethos (ns)	μέγεθος
skirt	i fusta (fs)	φούστα
socks	i kaltses (fp)	κάλτσες
statue	to agalma (ns)	άγαλμα
sweater	to zaketa (ns)	ζακέτα
swimsuit	to mayio (ns)	μαγιώ
towel	i petseta (fs)	πετσέτα
trousers	to panteloni (ns)	παντελόνι
T-shirt	to bluzaki (ns)	μπλουζάκι
try on (v)	thokimaso	δοκιμάσω
underwear	to esoruha (ns)	εσώρουχα
wear (v)	forao	φοράω
wool	to mali (ns)	μαλλί
zipper	to fermuar (ns)	φερμουάρ

Now here some useful phrases:

How much is it?	poso kani	Πόσο κάνει;
How much is one beer?	poso kani mia bira	Πόσο κάνει μια μπύρα.
The wine costs five euros.	to krasi kani pende evro	Το κρασί κάνει πέντε ευρώ.

Where can I buy ...	pu boro n'agoraso ...	Πού μπορώ να αγοράσω
Here you are.	oriste	Ορίστε.
Are the shops open?	ine ta magazia anikta	Είναι τα μαγάσια ανοικτά;
I'd like to buy ...	tha thela n'agoraso ...	Θα'θελα ν'αγοράσω ...
I'd like this/that. (point)	tha ithela avto/oti	Θα ήθελα αυτό/ότι.
I'd like one like that.	tha ithela ena tetio	Θα ήθελα ένα τέτοιο.
It's very cheap.	ine poli ftinos	Είναι πολύ φτηνός.
It's enough.	ine arketa	Είναι αρκετά.
It's too much.	ine para poli	Είναι πάρα πολύ.
It's very expensive.	ine poli akrivo	Είναι πολύ ακριβό.
It's too expensive.	ine para poli akrivo	Είναι πάρα πολύ ακριβό.
Is there a discount?	kanete ekptosi	Κάνετε έκπτωση;
Can I help you?	boro na sas voithiso	Μπορώ να σας βοηθήσω;
I can't.	then boro	Δεν μπορώ.
Where is the nearest bank?	pu ine i kondinoteri trapeza	Πού είναι η κοντινότερη τράπεζα;
I would like two postcards	tha ithela thio kartes	Θα ήθελα δύο κάρτες
Do you have ...?	ehete ...?	Έχετε ...;
Do you have maps of Athens?	ehete hartes tis athinas	Έχετε χάρτες της Αθήνας;
I'll have this.	tha paro avto	Θα πάρω αυτό
I would like to try on the dress.	tha ithela na thokimaso to forema	Θα ήθελα να δοκιμάσω το φόρεμα.
Can I try it on?	boro na to thokimaso ya	Μπορώ να το δοκιμάσω για;
Where can I try it on?	pu boro na to thikimasete	Μπορώ να το δοκιμάσετε;
My size is ...	to numero mu ine ...	Το νούμερό μου είναι ...

Do you have something larger?	ehete kati pio megalos	Έχετε κάτι πιό μεγάλος;
That's a lot.	ine poli	Είμαι πολύ.
I'm just looking.	ime apla psahnun	Είμαι απλά ψάχνουν
Here is the receipt.	oriste i apothixi	Όρίςτε η απόδειξη.
What do I owe you?	ti su hrostao	Τι σου χρωστάω;

Colors

Useful words for colors.

black	mavros	μαύρος
blue	ble	μπλε
brown	kafe	καφέ
gold	hrisos	χρυσός
gray	kri	γκρί
green	prasinos	πράσινος
orange	portokali	πσρτοκάλι
pink	roz	ροζ
purple	mov	μωβ
red	kokinos	κόκκινος
silver	asimi	ασήμι
stripped	riye	ριγέ
white	lefko	Λευκό
white	aspro	Άσπρο
yellow	kitrinos	κίτρινς
dark	skuros	σκούρος
light	anihtos	ανοιχτός

At the Pharmacy

Here are items that you can buy at the pharmacy farma<u>ki</u>o.

pharmacy	to farma<u>ki</u>o (ns)	φαρμακείο
pharmacist	o farmako<u>pios</u> (ms)	φαρμακοποιός
antiseptic	to antisepti<u>ko</u> (ns)	αντισηπτικό
antacid	to anti<u>ox</u>ino (ns)	αντιόξινο
aspirin	i aspi<u>ri</u>ni (fs)	ασπιρίνη
bandage	o epithesmos (ms)	επίδεσμος
cough	o <u>vi</u>has (ms)	βήχας
cough medication	to <u>vi</u>ha <u>farm</u>aka (ns)	βήχα φάρμακα
eyeglasses	ta ya<u>lia</u> (np)	γυαλιά
lipstick	to krayi<u>on</u> (ns)	κραγιόν
lotion	i losi<u>on</u> (fs)	λοσιόν
medication	to <u>farm</u>ako (ns)	φάρμακο
medicine	to iatri<u>ki</u> (ns)	ιατρική
pills	ta <u>ha</u>pia (np)	χάπια
prescription	i sinta<u>yi</u> (fs)	συνταγή
razor	to ksi<u>ra</u>fi (ns)	ξυράφι
shampoo	to sampu<u>an</u> (ns)	σαμπουάν
shaver	i ksiristi<u>ki</u> miha<u>ni</u> (fs)	ξυριστική μηχανή
soap	to sa<u>pu</u>ni (ns)	σαπούνι
sunburn	to ilia<u>ko</u> ekavma (ns)	ηλιακό έγκαυμα
sunglasses	ta yialia iliu (np)	γυαλιά ηλίου
sunblock	anti-ilia<u>ko</u>	αντιηλιακό
thermometer	to ther<u>mo</u>metro (ns)	θερμόμετρο
toilet paper	to harti iy<u>ias</u> (ns)	χαρτί υγείας
toothbrush	i orthon<u>do</u>vurtsa (fs)	οδοντόβουτσα
toothpaste	i orthon<u>do</u>pasta (fs)	οδοντόπαστα
toothpick	i othontoglif<u>i</u>da (fs)	οδοντογλυφίδα
towel	i pet<u>se</u>ta (fs)	πετσέτα

Activities in the Country

Visit the many beautiful sights in Greece. Here are some words to use when you are out sight-seeing, hiking or camping in the country.

backpack, knapsack	to sakithio (ns)	σακκίδιο
bay	o kolpos (ms)	κόλπος
beach	i paralia (fs)	παραλία
bicycle	to pothilato (ns)	ποδήλατο
boat	to varka (ns)	βάρκα
boat	to karavi (ns)	καράβι
bridge	i yefira (fs)	γέφυρα
campsite	to kamping (ns)	κάμπινγκ
canal	to kanali (ns)	κανάλι
candle	to keri (ns)	κερί
canoe	to kano (ns)	κανό
can, bottle opener	to anihtiri (ns)	ανοιχτήρι
cave	to spilia (ns)	σπηλιά
cliff	o gremos (ms)	γκρεμός
cloud	to sinefo (ns)	σύννεφο
compass	i pixitha (fs)	πυξίδα
dam	to fragma (ns)	φράγμα
desert	i erimo (fs)	έριμο
far	makria	μακριά
farm	to agrotima (ns)	αγρόκτημα
fence	i perifraxi (fs)	περίφραξη
fishing	i aliea (fs)	αλιεία
flashlight (torch)	o fakos (ms)	φακός
flower	to luludi (ns)	λουλούδι
fog	i omihli (fs)	ομίχλι
forest	to thasos (ns)	Θάσος
fuel	to kafsima (ns)	καύσιμα
garden	o kipos (ms)	κήπος
gorge	to faragi (ns)	φαράγγι
hail	to halazi (ns)	χαλάζι

highway	avtokinitothromo	αυτοκινιτόδρομο
hike (v)	haratsi	χαράτσι
hiker	o pesoporos (ms)	πεζοπόρος
hiking	pesoporia	πεζοπορία
hill	o lofos (ms)	λόφος
ice	o pagos (ms)	πάγος
island	to nisi (ns)	νησί
kilometre	hiliometro	χιλιώμετρο
lake	i limni (fs)	λίμνη
lighter	o anaptiras (ms)	αναπτήρας
lightning	i astrapi (fs)	αστραπή
map	o hartis (ms)	χάρτης
road map	o othikos hartis (ms)	οδικός χάρτης
matches	ta spirta (np)	σπίρτα
motorboat	to skafos (ns)	σκάφος
mountain	to vuno (ns)	βουνό
near	konda	κοντά
path	i thiathromi (fs)	διαδρομή
peak	i korifi (fs)	κορυφή
permit	i athia (fs)	άδεια
rain	i vrohi (fs)	βροχή
river	to potani (ns)	ποτάνι
road	o thromos (ms)	δρόμος
route	i thiathromi (fs)	διαδρομή
sea	i thalasa (fs)	θάλασσα
ship	to plio (ns)	πλοίο
sign	to pinakitha (ns)	πινακίδα
sleeping bag	o ipnosakos (ms)	υπνόσακος
snow	to hioni (ns)	χιόνι
star	to astra (ns)	άστρα
storm	i kategitha (ns)	καταιγίδα
summer	to kalokeri (ns)	καλοκαίρι
sun	o ilios (ms)	ήλιος
sunrise	i anatoli (fs)	ανατολή
sunset	thisi	δύση
swim (v)	kolibo	κολυμπώ
swimming	i kolimvisi (fs)	κολύμβηση
swim suit	to mayio (ns)	μαγιώ

temperature	i thermokrasia (fs)	θερμοκρασία
tent	i skini (fs)	Σκηνή
tree	to thendro (ns)	δύέντρο
trip	to taxithi (ns)	Ταξίδι
valley (fs)	i kilatha (fs)	κοιλάδα
vineyard (ms)	o ambelonas (ms)	αμπελώνας
winery	to inopi-ia (fs)	οινοποιία
waterfall	o katarahtis (ms)	καταράχτης
water bottle	to bukali neru (ns)	μπουκάλι νερού
weather	o keros (ms)	καιρός
well	to pigadi (ns)	πηγάδι
winter	o himonas (ms)	χειμώνας

Travelling by Car

Here are some useful words to help you on your way. These are probably more than you need but just in case.

accident	to atihima (ns)	ατύχημα
car	to avtokinito (ns)	αυτοκίνητο
battery	i bataria (fs)	μπαταρία
(fan) belt	to luri (ns)	λουρί
brake	to frenon (ns)	φρένον
clutch	o simblektis (ms)	συμπλέκτης
engine	o kinitiras (ms)	κινητήρας
fuel (gasoline)	i venzini (fs)	δενζίνι
gas/petrol station	pratirio venzinis	Πρατίριο δενζίνις
fuel pump	i antlia venzinis	αντλία δενζίνις
garage	to garaz (ns)	γκαράζ
gearbox	to kivotio tahititon (ns)	κιβώτιο ταχυτήτον
headlight	o provoleas (ms)	προβολέας
motorway	o avtokinito thromo (ms)	αυτοκινιτόδρομο
indicator	o thiktis (ms)	δείκτης

insurance	i asfalistiki (fs)	ασφαλιστική
key	to klithi (ns)	κλειδί
driver's license	athia othigisis	άδεια οδήγησης
map	o hartis (ms)	χάρτης
mechanic	o mihanikos (ms)	μηχανικός
oil	to petreleo (ns)	πετρέλαιο
parking	o stathmefsi (ms)	στάθμευση
police	astinomikos	αστινομικός
police station	astinomiko tmima	αστινομικό τμήμα
police officer	o astinomikos (ms)	αστινομικός
pump	i antlia (fs)	αντλία
puncture	i parakentisi (fs)	παρακέντηση
radiator	to psigio (ns)	ψυγείο
rent, hire (v)	nikiazo	νικιάζω
road	o thromos (ms)	δρόμος
screwdriver	to katsavithi (ns)	κατσαβίδι
starter	i miza (fs)	μίζα
steering wheel	to timoni (ns)	τιμόνι
tire	to lastiho (ns)	λάστιχο
tow truck	yeranos	γερανός
truck	to fortigo (ns)	φορτηγό
tunnel	i siraga (fs)	σήραγγα
van	to fortgali (ns)	φορτηγάλι
pump	i antlia neru (fs)	αντλία νερού
wheel	o trohos (ms)	τροχός
windshield	to pampriz (ns)	παρμπρίζ
wrench, spanner	to klithi (ns)	κλειδί

Here are some phrases to use. Don't forget to add please
parakalo!

I want to rent a car.	thelo na nikiaso ena avtokinito	Θέλω να νοικιάσω ένα αυτοκίνητο
Where can I buy gasoline?	pu boro n'agoraso venzini	Πού μπορώ να αγοράσω βενζίνη;
I have a credit card.	eho mia pistotiki karta	Έχω μια πιστωτική κάρτα.
How far is it?	poso makria ine	Πόσο μακριά είναι;
Where is the	pu ine to	Πού είναι το

nearest garage?	kond<u>i</u>n<u>o</u>tero g<u>ara</u>z	κοντινότερο γκαράζ;
Where is the nearest gas station?	pu <u>i</u>ne to kond<u>i</u>n<u>o</u>tero prat<u>i</u>rio ven<u>z</u>inis	Πού είναι το κοντινότερο πρατίριο δενζίνις;
Fill it up!	y<u>emi</u>ste to	Γεμίστε το!
Can you check the oil?	bor<u>i</u>te na el<u>eg</u>xete ta <u>l</u>athia	Μπορείτε να ελέγξετε τα λάδια;
Can you check the water?	bor<u>i</u>te na el<u>eg</u>xete to ne<u>ro</u>	Μπορείτε να ελέγξετε το νερό;
My car has broken down.	<u>h</u>alase to avto<u>ki</u>nito mu	Χάλααε το αυτοκίνητο μου.
Where does this road go?	pu <u>pai</u> avt<u>os</u> o <u>thro</u>mos	Πού πάει αυτός ο δρόμος;
Where is the road to ...?	pu <u>i</u>ne o <u>thro</u>mos ya ...	Πού είναι ο δρόμος για ...;
I have a puncture.	<u>tri</u>pise to <u>la</u>stiho	Τρύπησε τό λάστιχο.
Do you do repairs?	<u>k</u>anete episke<u>ve</u>s	Κάνετε έπισκευές;
I don't do repairs.	then <u>k</u>ano episke<u>ve</u>s	Δεν κάνω επισκευές.

Verbs - Imperative Tense (G)

Imperatives are requests or commands made to another person or persons. We have seen some already and we will cover several useful ones here. These come in two forms:

- singular, informal form (s)

- plural, formal form. (p)

As a visitor you will most likely use the formal, polite form. Here are some examples:

ask	<u>ro</u>tiste	ρωτήστε
bring	<u>fe</u>rete	φέρετε

close	kliste	κλείστε
come	elate	ελάτε
continue	sinehiste	συνεχίστε
drink	piite	πιείτε
eat	fate	φάτε
find	vrite	βρείτε
get, take	parete	πάρετε
get up	sikothite	σηκωθείτε
go	piyene	πήγαινε
go up	anethite	ανεβείτε
go down	katethite	κατεβείτε
give	thoste	δώστε
hear, listen	akuste	ακούστε
look	kitakste	κυττάξτε
open	anixte	ανοίξτε
put	valte	βάλτε
read	thiavaste	διαβάστε
repeat	epanalavete	επαναλάβετε
run	trexe	τρέξε
say, tell me	pite	πίτε
sit	kathiste	καθίστε
speak	miliste	μιλήστε
stay	minete	μείνετε
take	parete	πάρετε
turn	stripste	στρίψτε
wait	perimenete	περιμένετε
write	grapste	γράψτε

Here are some examples:

Sit please.	kathiste parakalo	Καθίστε παρακαλώ.
Listen again.	akuste ksana	Ακούστε ξανά.
Tell me something.	pite mu kati	Πίτε μου κάτι.
Speak slower.	miliste pio arga	Μιλήστε πιο αργά.
Come to my house (place).	elate sto spiti mu	Έλάτε στο σπίτι μου.
Take us!	parete mas	Πάρετε μας!

Take this!	parete avto	Πάρετε αυτό!
Go straight.	piyene evthia	Πήγαινε ευθεία.
Turn right at the corner.	stripste thexia sto gonia	Στρίψτε δεξιά στη γωνία.
Stay at the hotel Nikis.	minete sto'ksenodohio nikis	Μείνετε στο ξενοδοχείο Νίκης.
Don't touch.	min angizete	μην αγγίζετε.
Open the book.	anixte to vivlio	Ανοίξτε το βιβλίο.

Difficulties

When travelling you may encounter problems, hopefully not. First some important phone numbers in Greece.

Police	astinomia	100
Ambulance	asthenoforo	166
Fire Service	pirosvestiki ipiresia	199
Tourist Police	turistiki astinomia	171

Here are some words that may help.

accident	to atihima (ns)	ατύχημα
ankle	o astragalo (ms)	αστράγαλο
appointment	to randevu (ns)	ραντεβού
arm	to heri (ns)	χέρι
back	i plati (fs)	πλάτη
bandage	o epithesmos (ns)	επίδεσμος
body	to soma (ns)	σώμα
bone	to osto (ns)	οστό
burn	to enkavma (ns)	έγκαυμα
chest	to stithos (ns)	στήθος
contact lenses	i faki epafis (fs)	φακοί επαφής
cough	o vihas (ms)	βήχας
ear	to avti (ns)	αυτί
eye	to mati (ns)	μάτι

doctor	o ya<u>tros</u> (ms)	γιατρός
dentist	o othon<u>di</u>atros (ns)	οδοντίατρος
difficulty	i thiskolia (fs)	δυσκολία
embassy	i pres<u>vi</u>a (fs)	πρεσβεία
emergency	e<u>pi</u>gon	επείγον
face	to <u>pro</u>sopo (ns)	πρόσοπο
fever	o pire<u>tos</u> (ms)	πυρετός
finger	to <u>tha</u>htilo (ns)	δάχτυλο
first aid	<u>pro</u>tes voi<u>thi</u>es	πρώτες βοήθειες
flu	i <u>gri</u>pi (fs)	γρίπη
handbag	i <u>tsa</u>nda (fs)	τσάντα
leg	to <u>po</u>thi (ns)	πόδι
hand	to <u>he</u>ri (ns)	χέρι
head	to ke<u>fa</u>li (ns)	κεφάλι
headache	to pono<u>ke</u>falo (ns)	πονοκέφαλο
heart	i karthi<u>a</u> (fs)	καρδιά
hospital	to nosoko<u>mi</u>o (ns)	νοσοκομείο
infection	i <u>mo</u>linsi (fs)	μόλυνση
injection	i <u>e</u>nesi (fs)	ένεση
knee	to <u>go</u>nato (ns)	γόνατο
medication	to <u>fa</u>rmako (ns)	φάρμακο
mouth	to <u>sto</u>ma (ns)	στόμα
nausea	i navtia (fs)	ναυτία
nose	i <u>mi</u>ti (fs)	μύτη
neck	o le<u>mos</u> (ms)	λαιμός
nurse	o noso<u>ko</u>mos (ms)	ο νοσοκόμος
nurse	i nosoko<u>ma</u> (fs)	η νοσοκόμα
pain	o <u>po</u>nos (ms)	πόνος
painkillers	ta anali<u>ti</u>ka (np)	αναλγητικά
pharmacy	to farma<u>ki</u>o (ns)	φαρμακείο
pills	ta <u>ha</u>pia (np)	χάπια
police	i astino<u>mi</u>a (fs)	αστυνομία
police station	to astinomi<u>ko</u> t<u>mi</u>ma (ns)	αστινομικό τμήμα
police officer	o astinomi<u>kos</u> (ms)	αστυνόμος
prescription	i sinta<u>yi</u> (fs)	συνταγή
problem	to pro<u>vli</u>ma (ns)	πρόβλιμα
pulse	o sfig<u>mos</u> (ms)	σφυγμός
safety	i as<u>fa</u>lia (fs)	ασφάλεια

sick	arostos	άρρωστος
sore throat	to ponolemos (ns)	πονόλαιμος
stomach	to stomahi (ns)	στομάχι
sore	apoyevma	απόγευμα
thirsty	thipsasmenos	διψασμένος
tongue	i glosa (fs)	γλώσσα
tooth	to thonti (ns)	δόντι
throat	to lemos (ns)	λαιμός
urgent	epigon	επείγων
vacination	to emvolio (ns)	εμβόλιο
valuable	politimos	πολύτιμος
wallet	to portofoli (ns)	πορτοφόλι
X-ray	i aktinografia (fs)	ακτινογραφία

These phrases may also help.

Can you help me?	borite na voithisete	μπορείτε να με βοηθήσετε;
Is something wrong?	iparhi kati lathos	Υπάρχει κάτι λάθος;
What's the matter?	ti simveni	Τι σιμβένι;
There was a road accident.	ipirhe ena atihima	Υπήρχε ένα ατύχημα
I'm lost.	hanome	Χάνομαι
Help!	voithia	Βοήθεια!
Go away!	fiye	Φύγε!
I'm ok.	ime endaxi	Είμαι εντάξει.
I've been injured.	eho travmaties	Έχω τραυματίες.
I'm sick.	ime arostos	Είμαι άρρωστος.
My wallet has been stolen.	eklapi to portofoli mu	Εκλάπη το πορτοφόλι μου.
It was stolen.	ihe klapi	Είχε κλαπεί.
I lost my passport.	ehasa to thiavatirio mu	Έχασα το διαβατήριό μου.
I need a doctor.	hriazome ena yatro	Χρειάζομε ένα γιατρό.
I have a headache	eho ena	Έχω ένα

	ponokefalo	πονοκέφαλο
I have a fever.	eho pireto	Έχω πυρετό.
I feel dizzy.	niotho zalada	Νιώθω ζαλάδα.
I have diabetes.	eho thiaviti	Έχω διαβήτη.
I have a toothache.	eho ponothondo	Έχω πονόδοντο.
I have high blood pressure.	eho ipsili artiriaki piesi	Έχω υψηλή αρτηριακή πίεση.
Open your mouth.	anixte to stoma sas	Ανοίξτε το στόμα σας.
Are you allergic to anything?	iste aleryikise kati	Είστε αλλεργικοί σε κάτι;
Where does it hurt?	opu ponai	όπου πονάει;
Breathe deeply.	anapnevste vathia	Αναπνεύστε βαθιά.

Adverbs (G)

Most Greek adverbs are similar to adjectives but with a different prefix or suffix in the same way as English. For example, the adjective 'quick' becomes the adverb 'quickly'. Unlike adjectives, Greek adverbs have only one form.

Here is a list of commonly used adverbs.

always	pantote	πάντοτε
carefully	prosektika	προσεκτικά
early	noris	νορίς
exactly	akrivos	ακριβός
finally	telika	τελικά
gladly	efharistos	ευχαρίστως
here	etho	εδώ
immediately	amesos	αμέσος
lately	prosfaka	πρόσφατα
never	pote	ποτέ
nicely	omorfa	όμορφα
properly	theondos	δεόντως

quickly, fast	grigora	γρήγορα
rarely	spania	σπάνια
regularly	taktika	Τακτικά
slightly	elafros	ελαφρώς
slowly	arga	αργά
soon	sintoma	σύντομα
then	tote	τότε
there	eki	εκεί
up	pano	πάνω
well, nicely	kala	καλά

Signs

Here is a list of signs that you may encounter in Greece.

ΑΝΟΙΧΤΟ	anihto	Open
ΑΡΓΑ	arga	Slow
ΑΠΑΓΟΡΕΥΕΤΑΙ Η ΦΩΤΟΓΡΑΦΗΣΗ	apayorevete i fotografisi	No photography (forbidden)
ΑΠΑΓΟΡΕΥΕΤΑΙ Η ΣΤΑΘΜΕΥΣΙΣ	apayorevete i stathmevsis	No parking (forbidden)
ΑΠΑΓΟΡΕΥΕΤΑΙ Η ΕΙΣΟΔΟΣ	apayorevete i isothos	No entry (forbidden)
ΑΠΑΓΟΡΕΥΕΤΑΙ ΤΟ ΚΑΠΝΙΣΜΑ	apayorevete to kapinisma	No smoking (forbidden)
ΑΝΑΜΕΙΝΑΤΕ	anaminate	Wait
ΑΠΟΧΩΡΗΤΗΡΙΑ	apohritiria	Toilets
ΑΝΔΡΩΝ	andron	Men's
ΓΥΝΑΙΚΩΝ	yinekon	Women's
ΑΣΤΥΝΟΜΙΑ	astinomia	Police
ΒΙΒΛΙΟΠΩΛΕΙΟ	vivliopolio	Bookshop
ΓΡΑΜΜΑΤΟΣΗΜΑ	gramatosima	Stamps

ΙΔΙΩΤΙΚΟΣ ΧΩΡΟΣ	ithiotikos horos	Private area
ΚΛΕΙΣΤΟ	klisto	Closed
ΕΙΣΟΔΟΣ	isothos	Entrance
ΕΞΟΔΟΣ	exothos	Exit
ΕΙΣΙΤΗΡΙΑ	isitiria	Tickets
ΔΙΟΔΙΑ	thiothia	Toll
ΚΙΝΔΥΝΟΣ	kinthinos	Danger
ΜΗΝ ΑΓΓΙΖΕΤΕ	min engizete	Do not touch
ΝΟΣΟΚΟΜΕΙΟ	nosokomio	Hospital
ΟΔΗΓΟΣ	othigos	Guide
ΕΟΤ	elinikos organismos turismu	Greek Tourist Office
ΟΛΠ	organismos limenos pireos	Piraeus Port Authority
ΣΝΑΚΣ	snacks	Snacks
ΣΤΑΣΙ ΛΕΩΦΟΡΙΟΥ	stasi leoforio	Bus stop
ΣΤΑΣΗ ΤΡΟΛΛΕΥ	stasi troli	Trolley stop
ΣΥΡΑΤΕ	sirate	Push
ΟΘΗΣΑΤΕ	othisate	Pull
ΤΟΥΑΛΕΤΕΣ	toyaletes	Toilets
ΠΕΙΡΑΙΑΣ	pireas	Piraeus
ΣΩΣΙΒΙΑ	sosivia	Life jackets
ΧΑΛΑΣΜΕΝΟ	halasmeno	Out of order
ΦΑΞ	fax	Fax

Wrap Up

I hope you have enjoyed your introduction to Greek using this guide. This should only be the start of your journey to conversing in Greek. Once you have made some progress in speaking Greek and have mastered a small vocabulary you should start to read Greek text. There are many resources available to help you with that.

English - Greek Dictionary

All verbs are marked as (v) and are shown in the first person singular of the present tense. The imperative (command) form of a verb is marked as (vi).

Nouns are shown with the definite article and their gender. For example,

man o **anthras** (ms)	άνδρας
woman i **yineka** (fs)	γυναίκα
house **to** **spiti** (ns)	σπίτι

A

a.m. **pi-mi**	π.μ.
about **peripu**	περίπου
accept (v) **apothehome**	αποδέχομαι
accident **to** **atihima** (ns)	ατύχημα
accommodation **i thiamoni** (fs)	διαμονή
adapter **o proseramogea** (ms)	προσαμογέα
address **i thiefthinsi** (fs)	διεύθυνση
adjacent **thipla**	δίπλα
advice **i simbules** (fs)	συμβολές
afternoon **to apoyevma** (ns)	απόγευμα
again **ksana**	ξανά
air **o aera** (ms)	αέρα
air conditioning **o klimatismu** (ms)	κλιματισμού
air conditioner **to klimatisko** (ns)	κλιματισκό
airplane **to aeroplano** (ns)	αεροπλάνο
airport **to erothromio** (ns)	αεροδρόμιο
aisle, row **to thiathromo** (ns)	διάδρομο
all, everything **ola**	όλα
almonds **ta amythala** (np)	αμύγδαλα
almost **shethon**	σχεδόν
already **ithi**	ήδη
also **episis**	επίσης
always **pantote**	πάντοτε

and	**ke**	και
ankle	**o astragalo** (ms)	αστράγαλο
answer	**i apanthisi** (fs)	απάνδισι
apartment	**to thiamerisma** (ns)	διαμέρισμα
apple	**to milo** (ns)	μίλο
apricot	**to verikoko** (ns)	βερίκοκο
Arabic	**aravikos**	αραβικός
arrive	(v) **ftano**	φτάνω
ask	(v) **zito**	ζητώ
at	**stis**	στις
aunt	**i thia** (fs)	θεία
avenue	**i leoforos** (fs)	λεωφόρος

B

backpack	**to sakithio** (ns)	σακίδιο
bad	**kakos**	κακός
baggage	**i aposkeves** (fp)	αποσκευές
bakery	**to artopolio** (ns)	αρτοπωλείο
balcony	**to balkoni** (ns)	μπαλκόνι
ball	**i bala** (fs)	μπάλα
banana	**i banana** (fs)	μπανάνα
bank	**i trapeza** (fs)	τράπεζα
basket	**to kalathi** (ns)	καλάθι
bathtub	**i baniera** (fs)	μπανιέρα
battery	**i bataria** (fs)	μπαταρία
beach	**i paralia** (fs)	παραλία
because	**yati**	γιατί
bed	**to krevati** (ns)	κρεβάτι
to be	(v) **ime**	είμαι
bee	**i melisa** (fs)	μέλισσα
beer	**i bira** (fs)	μπύρα
between	**metaxi**	μεταξύ
bible	**i biblios** (fs)	βίβλιος
bicycle	**to pothilato** (ns)	ποδίλατο
big	**megalos**	μεγάλος
binoculars	**ta kialia** (np)	κιάλια
bird	**to pouli** (ns)	πουλί
birthday	**yenethlion**	γενεθλιον
black	**mavro**	μαύρος
blanket	**i kuverta** (fs)	κουβέρτα
blue	**ble**	μπλε

boat **to karavi** (ns)   καράβι
body **to soma** (ns)   σώπα
bone **to oston** (ns)   οστών
book **to vivlio** (ns)   βιβλίο
bookstore **to vivliopolio** (ns)   βιβλιοπωλείο
bottle **to bukali** (ns)   μπουκάλι
bottle opener **to anahtiri** (ns)   ανοιχτήρι
boy **to agori** (ns)   αγόρι
box **to kuti** (ns)   κουτι
brake **to frenon** (ns)   φρένον
bread **to psomi** (ns)   ψωμί
breakfast **to proino** (ns)   προινό
bridge **i yefira** (fs)   γέφιρα
brother **o athelfos** (ms)   αδελφός
brown **kafe**   καφέ
building **to ktirio** (ns)   κτιρίο
bus **to leoforio** (ns)   λεωφορείο
bus stop **i stasi leoforio** (fs)   στάσι λεωφορείο
business **i epihirison** (fs)   επιχειρήσεων
busy **apasholimenos**   απασχοληµένος
but **ala**   αλλά
butter **to vutiro** (ns)   βούτυρο
buttons **ta kubia** (np)   κουµπιά
buy (v) **agorazo**   αγοράζω

C

cake **to kake** (ns)   κέικ
calculator **i arithmonihani** (fs)   αριθµονηχανη
camera **i kamera** (fs)   κάµερα
campsite **to kamping** (ns)   κάµπινγκ
camping **kamping**   κάµπινγκ
canal **o kanali** (ms)   κανάλι
canoe **to kano** (ns)   κανό
carrot **to karoto** (ns)   καρότο
car **to avtokinito** (ns)   αυτοκίνητο
castle **to kastro** (ns)   κάστρο
cat **i gata** (fs)   γάτα
caution **prosohi**   προσοχή
cave **to spileo** (ns)   σπίλαιο
cellphone **to kiniti tilefono** (ns)   κινιτή τηλέφωνο

center **to kentro** (ns)	κέντρο
chair **i karekla** (fs)	καρέκλα
cheap **ftino**	φτηνό
cheese **to tiri** (ns)	τυρί
chicken **to kotopulo** (ns)	κοτόπουλο
child **to pethi** (ns)	παιδί
children **ta pethia** (np)	παιδιά
chocolate **sokolata**	σοκολάτα
church **i eklisia** (fs)	εκκλησία
circle **o kiklos** (ms)	κύκλος
city **i poli** (fs)	πόλι
class **i katigoria** (fs)	καταγορία
clean **katharos**	καθαρός
clock **to roloi** (ns)	ρολόι
close (v) **klino**	κλείνω
closed **klistos**	κλείστός
cliff **o nkremo** (ms)	γκρεμό
cloud **to sinefo** (ns)	σύννεφο
coast **i paralia** (fs)	παραλία
coat **to palto** (ns)	παλτό
coffee **o kafes** (ms)	καφές
cold **krio**	κρύο
come (v) **erhome**	έρχομαι
comb **i htena** (fs)	χτένα
compass **i pixida** (fs)	πυξίδα
computer **ipoloyisti**	υπολογιστή
congratulations **sinharitiria**	συγχαρήταρια
consulate **to proxenio** (ns)	προξενείο
continue (v) **snehizo**	συνεχίζω
conversation **sinomilia**	συνομιλία
cookie **to biskoto** (ns)	μπισκότο
cool **throseros**	δροσερός
corn **to kalamboki** (ns)	καλαμπόκι
corner **i gonia** (fs)	γονία
cosmetics **ta kalandika** (np)	καλλυντικά
count (v) **arithmo**	αριθμώ
country **i hora** (fs)	χώρα
couple **to zevgari** (ns)	ζευγάρι
cow **i ayelatha** (fs)	αγελάδα
crafts **i hirotehnia** (fp)	χιροεχνία
cross (religious) **o stavros** (ms)	σταυρός
cucumber **to aguri** (ns)	αγγούρι

D

danger **kinthinos**	κίνδυνος
dangerous **epikinthinos**	επικίνδυνος
day i **mera** (fs)	μέρα
daughter i **kori** (fs)	κόρι
deep **vathis**	βαθύς
delicatessen i **alandika** (fs)	αλαντικά
delicious **nostima**	νόστιμα
dentist o/i **odontiatro** (MS/FS)	οδοντίατρο
desert i **erimo** (fs)	έριμο
different **thiaforetikos**	διαφορεικός
difficult **thiskolos**	δυσκολός
difficulty **thiskolia**	δυσκολία
dinner **to vrathino** (ns)	βραδινό
direction i **katefunsi** (fs)	κατεύφυνση
dirty **vromikos**	βρώμικος
discount **ekptosi**	έκπτωση
do (v) **kano**	κάνω
doctor o/i **yatros** (ms/fs)	γιατρός
dog o **skilos** (ms)	σκύλος
door **apo**	από
door i **porta** (fs)	πόρτα
down **kato**	κάτω
dress **to forema** (ns)	φόρεμα
drink (v) **pino**	πίνω
drive (v) **odivo**	οδηγω
driver o **odivu** (ms)	οδηγού
dry **ksiros**	ξηρός

E

ear **to avti** (ns)	αυτί
early **noris**	νορίς
early **evkolos**	εύκολος
east i **anatolika** (fs)	ανατολικά
eat (v) **fao**	φάω
electric outlet i **priza** (fs)	πρίζα
electricity **elektrismos**	ηλεκτρισμός

egg **to av<u>go</u>** (ns)	αυγό
eggplant **i meli<u>tzana</u>** (fs)	μελιτζάνα
elevator **to anelki<u>stiras</u>** (ns)	ανελκυστήρας
embassy **i pres<u>via</u>** (fs)	πρεσβεία
end **to <u>telos</u>** (ns)	τέλος
English **angli<u>ka</u>**	Αγγλικά
enough **arke<u>ta</u>**	αρκετά
entrance **i <u>isothos</u>** (fs)	είσοδος
envelope **o <u>fakelos</u>** (ms)	φάκελος
eraser **i <u>goma</u>** (fs)	γόμα
euro **ev<u>ro</u>**	ευρώ
evening **to <u>vrathi</u>** (ns)	βράδυ
every **<u>kathe</u>**	κάθε
everywhere **pan<u>du</u>**	παντού
exactly **akri<u>vos</u>**	ακριβός
example **to pa<u>radigma</u>** (ns)	παράδειγμα
excellent **<u>aristi</u>**	άριστη
excuse me **sig<u>nomi</u>**	συγγνώμη
exit **i <u>ex</u>othos** (fs)	έξοδος
expensive **akri<u>va</u>**	ακριβά
eye **to <u>mati</u>** (ns)	μάτι
eyeglasses **ta yali<u>a</u>** (np)	γυαλιά

F

face **to pro<u>so</u>po** (ns)	πρόσοπο
family **i iko<u>yeni</u>a** (fs)	οικογένεια
far **<u>simera</u>**	σήμερα
fast **<u>grigora</u>**	γρήγορα
father **o pa<u>teras</u>** (ms)	πατέρας
feel (v) **ais<u>than</u>ondai**	αισθάνονται
ferry **to plo<u>io</u>** (ns)	πλοίο
fig **ik**	εικ
find (v) **<u>vrisko</u>**	βρίσκω
finger **to <u>thahtilo</u>** (ns)	δάχτιλο
fire **i foti<u>a</u>** (fs)	φωτιά
fish **to <u>psari</u>** (ns) **<u>psaria</u>** (np)	ψάρι
flashlight **o <u>fako</u>** (ms)	φάκο
flight **i <u>ptisi</u>** (fs)	πτήση
flower **to lul<u>udi</u>** (ns)	λουλούδι
food **tro<u>fimon</u>**	τροφίμον
forbidden **apayo<u>revete</u>**	απαγορεύεται

97

fork to pi**ru**ni (ns)	πιρούνι
free of charge **tz**a**ba**	τζάμπα
free of charge **thorean**	δωρεάν
French **yalika**	Γαλλικά
friend **fi**los (ms)	φίλος
friend **fili** (fs)	φίλι
from a**po**	από
fruit **fru**to	φρούτο
fuel, gasoline kaf**sim**on	καυσίμον
full ye**ma**tos	γεμάτος

G

garage to ga**raz** (ns)	γκαράζ
garden o **kip**os (ms)	κήπος
garlic to **skor**tho (ns)	σκόρδο
gasoline i ven**zi**ni (fs)	δενζίνι
gift **to do**ro (ns)	δώρο
girl to ko**rit**si (ns)	κορίτσι
give (v) **thi**no	δίνω
glass to po**ti**ri (ns)	ποτήρι
gloves ta **ganthia** (np)	γάνδια
go (v) pi**yen**o	πηγαίνω
goat i **katsika** (fs)	κατσίκα
good ka**los**	καλός
goodbye a**thi**o	αντίο
goodbye ya sas (plural, formal)	γεια σας
goodbye ya su (singular)	γεια σου
grandmother i **yaya** (fs)	γιαγιά
grandfather o **papus** (ms)	παππούς
grandchild/daughter engo**ni** (fs)	εγγονή
grandson o engo**nos** (ms)	εγγονός
grape to sta**fi**li (ns)	σταφύλι
grapefruit **grapefruit**	γκρέιπφρουτ
Greek eleni**ka**	ελληνικά
green **prasi**nos	πράσινος
guest o episki**pton** (ms)	επισκεπών
guide o othi**gos** (ms)	οδηγός

H

half mi**sos**	μισός
hamburger hamburker	χάμπουργκερ
hand to **heri** (ns)	χέρι
handbag i **tsanda** (fs)	τσάντα
hanger i kre**mastra** (fs)	κρεμάστρα
happy evtihis**menos**	ευτυχισμένος
hat **ehi**	έχει
have (v) **eho**	έχω
he au**tos**	αυτός
head to ke**fali** (ns)	κεφάλι
headlight o provo**leon** (ms)	προβολέον
headphones ta akusti**ka** (np)	ακουστικά
hear (v) ak**uo**	ακούω
heart i kardi**a** (fs)	καρδιά
heating the**rmasi**	θέρμασι
hello ya su	γεια σου
hello **herete**	χαίρετε
help voi**thisi**	βοηθήσει
here e**tho**	εδώ
high psi**lo**	ψηλό
highway o avtokini**tothromo** (ms)	αυτοκινιτόδρομο
hiking pezopo**ria**	πεζοπορία
home, house i **spiti** (ns)	σπίτι
homemade **spitikos**	σπιτικός
hospital to nosoko**mio** (ns)	νοσοκομείο
hostel o ze**nonas** (ms)	ζενώνας
hot kav**to**	καυτό
hotel to ksenodo**hio** (ns)	ξενοδοχείο
hour **ora**	ώρα
how? pos	Πός;
how are you? pos **iste**	Πώς είστε;
how much? **posos**	πόσος;
husband an**thras**	άνδρας

I

I e**go**	εγώ

icecream **to pago<u>to</u>** (ns)	παγωτό
if **an**	αν
information **i pliroforﾠ<u>ies</u>** (fs)	πληροφορίες
injection **i <u>en</u>esi** (fs)	ένεση
it **to**	το
important **simandi<u>ko</u>**	σημαντικό
immediately **am<u>es</u>os**	αμέσος
inexpensive **a<u>nex</u>othi**	ανέξοδη

J

jelly, jam **<u>ores</u>**	ώρες
job **i thulia** (fs)	δουλειά
journey **to taxithi** (ns)	ταξίδι
juice **o hi<u>mos</u>** (ms)	χυπός

K

key **to kli<u>thi</u>** (ns)	κλειδί
kiosk **to per<u>ip</u>tero** (ns)	περίπτερο
kitchen **i ku<u>zi</u>na** (fs)	κουζίνα
knee **to <u>gon</u>ato** (ns)	γόνατο
knife **to ma<u>her</u>i** (ns)	μαχαίρι
know (v) **<u>ksero</u>**	ξέρω

L

lake **i <u>lim</u>ni** (fs)	λίμνη
lamb **to ar<u>ni</u>** (ns)	αρνί
lamp **i <u>lam</u>pa** (fs)	λάμπα
land **i gi** (fs)	γη
language **i <u>glos</u>a** (ns)	γλώσσα
late **ar<u>ga</u>**	αργά

later **argotera**   αργότερα
laundry **to plintirio** (ns)   πλυντήριο
learn (v) **matheno**   μαθαίνω
leave (v) **afino**   αφήνω
left **to aristera** (ns)   αριστερά
leg **to pothi** (ns)   πόδι
lemon **to lemoni** (ns)   λεμόνι
length **to mikos** (ns)   μήκος
less **mion**   μείον
letter (mail) **i epistoli** (fs)   επιστολή
life **zoi**   ζωή
lightbulb **glombos**   γλόμπος
love (v) **agapo**   αγαπώ
line **i grami** (fs)   γραμμή
live, reside (v) **meno**   μένω
living room **saloni**   σαλόνι
a little **ligo** (ms), **ligi** (fs), **ligo** (ns)   λίγο
loaf **to karveli** (ns)   καρβέλι
lobby **ethousa**   αίθουσα
long **makris**   μακρύς
luggage **i aposkeves** (fp)   αποσκευές
lunch **to mesimeriano** (ns)   μεσημεριαό

M

magazine **to periothiko** (ns)   περιοδικό
mail **to tahithromio** (ns)   ταχυδρομείο
make (v) **ftiahno**   φτιάχνω
man **o anthras** (ms)   άνδρας
many **pola**   πολλά
map **o hartis** (ms)   χάρτης
market **i agora** (fs)   αγορά
matches **ta spirta** (np)   σπίρτα
maybe **isos**   ίσος
meal **to yevma** (ns)   γεύμα
medication **to farmako** (ns)   φάρμακο
menu **to menu** (ns)   μενού
midday **to mesimera** (ns)   μεσημέρι
middle **mesi**   μέση
milk **to gala** (ns)   γάλα
minute **ena lepto**   λεπτό
mirror **o kathreftis** (ms)   καθρέφτης

money **ta hrimata** (np)	χρίπατα
money **ta lefta** (np)	λεφτά
month **o minas** (ms)	μήνας
more **pio**	πιο
more **perisotero**	περισσότερο
morning **to proi** (ns)	πρωί
mother **i mitera** (fs)	μητέρα
motorcycle **i motosikleta** (fs)	μοτοσυκλέτα
mountain **to vuno** (ns)	βουνό
movie **i tenia** (fs)	ταινία
Mr. **o kirios**	κύριος
Mrs. **i kiria**	κυρία
Miss **thespinis**	δεσποινίς
museum **to musio** (ns)	μουσείο
mushroom **to manitari** (ns)	μανιτάρι
must (v) **prepi**	πρερι

N

name **to onoma** (ns)	όνομα
near **kondinos**	κοντινός
need (v) **hriazome**	χρειάζομαι
neighbour **o yitonas** (ms)	γείτονας
nephew **o anipsios** (ms)	ανιψιός
new **neos**	νέος
newspaper **i efimeritha** (fs)	εφημερίδα
next **epomenos**	επόμενος
nice **oreos**	ορέος
niece **i anipsia** (fs)	ανιψιά
night **i nihta** (fs)	νύχτα
no **ohi**	όχι
not **then**	δεν
noise **o thorios** (ms)	θόρυβος
noon **to mesimeri** (ns)	μεσημέρι
north **voria**	βόρεια
notebook **to simiomatario** (ns)	σημειωματάριο
nothing **tipota**	τίποτα
now **tora**	τώρα
number **o arithmos** (ms)	αριθμός
nurse **i nosokoma** (fs)	νοσοκόμα
nurse **o nosokomos** (ms)	νοσοκόμος

O

of **tou**	του
office **to grafio** (ns)	γραφείο
often **suhna**	συχνά
oil **to lathi** (ns)	λάδι
ok **endaxi**	εντάξει
old **paleos**	παλαιός
olive **i elia** (fs)	ελιά
olive oil **to eleolatho** (ns)	ελαιόλαδο
onion **to kremithi** (ns)	κρεμμύδι
only **mono**	μόνο
opposite **apenanti**	απέναντι
orange **to portokali** (ns)	πορτοκάλι
outside **exo**	έξω
oven **o furnos** (ms)	φούρνος
owe (v) **hrostao**	χρωστάω

P

p.m. **mi-mi**	μ.μ.
pain **o ponos** (ms)	πόνος
pair **to zevgos** (ns)	ζεύγος
paper **to harti** (ns)	χαρτί
parents **i gonis** (fs)	γονείς
parking **stathmefsi**	στάθμευση
parking meter **parkometro**	παρκόμετρο
passenger **o/i epivatis** (MS/FS)	επιβάτης
passport **to thiavatirio** (ns)	διαβατήριο
pay (v) **plirono**	πληρώνω
pea **kefali**	κεφάλι
peach (ns) **to rothakino**	ροδάκινο
pear **ahladi**	αχλάδι
pen **to stilo** (ns)	στυλό
pencil **to molini** (ns)	μολύβι
people **i anthropi** (fs)	άνθρωποι

perhaps **isos**	ίσως
personal computer **o ipologisti** (ms)	υπολογιστή
pharmacy **to farmakio** (ns)	φαρμακείο
photograph **i fotografia** (fs)	φωτογραφία
pillow **to maxilari** (ns)	μαξιλάρι
pineapple **ananas**	ανανάς
pink **roz**	ροζ
place **to tropos** (ns)	τόπος
plate **to piato** (ns)	πιάτο
platform **i platform** (fs)	πλατφόρμα
pleasant **efharistos**	ευχάριστος
please **parakalo**	παρακαλώ
plum **to damaskino** (ns)	δαμάσκηνο
pocket **tsepi**	τσέπη
police officer **i astinomia** (fs)	αστινομία
police officer **o astinomikos** (ms)	αστινομικός
police station **astinomiko tmima**	αστυνομικό τμήμα
possibly **pithanos**	πιθανώς
postcard **kart postal**	καρτ ποστάλ
post office **to tahithromio** (ns)	ταχυδρομείο
prefer (v) **protimao**	προτιμάω
prepare (v) **etimazo**	ετοιμάζω
prescription **i sintayi** (fs)	συνταγή
price **i timi** (fs)	τιμή
printer **o ektipotis** (ms)	εκτυπωτής
problem **to provlina** (ns)	πρόβλιμα
pronunication **to profora** (ns)	προφορά
pulse **o sfigmos** (ms)	σφυγμός
puncture **i parakentisi** (fs)	παρακέντηση

Q

quarter **tetarto**	τέταρτο
question **to erotisi** (ns)	ερώτηση
quickly **grigora**	γρήγορα
quiet **isiha**	ήσυχα

R

rain i vro**hi** (fs)	βροχή
raisin i sta**fitha** (fs)	σταφίδα
rarely **spa**nia	σπάνια
read (v) thia**va**so	διαβάσω
ready **eti**mos	έτοιμος
receipt i parala**vi** (fs)	παραλαβή
receive (v) lam**va**no	λαμβάνω
reception epithi**ho**	εποδοχή
red **ko**kinos	κόκκινος
refrigerator to psi**gio** (ns)	ψυγείο
rent (v) niki**azo**	νοικιάζω
reservation i **kra**tisi (fs)	κράτηση
rest a**na**pafsi	ανάπαυση
restaurant to estia**to**rio (ns)	εστιατόριο
restroom to **ba**nio (ns)	μπάνιο
rice to **ri**zi (ns)	ρύζι
right the**xia**	δεξιά
right (adj) the**xi**	δεξί
river o pota**mos** (ms)	ποταμός
room to tho**ma**tio (ns)	δωμάτιο
round strongi**los**	στρογγυλός
ruins ta e**ri**pia (np)	ερείπια

S

salad i sa**la**ta (fs)	σαλάτα
salt to a**la**ti (ns)	αλάτι
sandals ta san**da**lia (np)	σανδάλια
sale/discount i **ek**ptosi (fs)	έκπώληση
salesman o poli**tis** (ms)	πωλητής
saleswoman i po**li**tria (fs)	πωλήτρια
Saturday **sa**vvato	Σάββατο
sauce i **sal**tsa (fs)	σάλτσα
say (v) **le**o	λέω
scarf to kash**kol** (ns)	κασκόλ
school to skolio (ns)	σχολείο
sea i **tha**lasa (fs)	θάλασσα

see (v) vlepo	βλέπω
send (v) stelno	στέλνω
shampoo sampuan	σαμπουάν
shaver ksiristiki mihani	ξυριστική μηχανή
she avti	αυτή
ship to plio (ns)	πλοίο
shirt to pukamiso (ns)	πουκάμισο
shoe to papoutsi (ns)	παπούτσι
shorts ta sorts (np)	σορτς
shower to duz (ns)	ντους
sidewalk to pezothromia (ns)	πεζοδρόμιο
sign i pinakitha (fs)	πινακίδα
signature i pografo (fs)	υπογράφω
simple aplos	απλός
sing (v) tragutho	τραγουδώ
sit (v) kathome	κάθομαι
sister i adelfi (fs)	αδελφή
size meyethos	μέγεθος
skirt i fusta (fs)	φούστα
sky o uranos (ms)	ουρανός
slice i feta (fs)	φέτα
small mikros	μικρός
snack to snak (ns)	σνακ
as much to idio	το ίδιο
soap to sapuni (ns)	σαπούνι
soccer podosfero	ποδόσφαιρο
socks i kaltses (np)	κάλτσες
sofa p kanapes (ms)	καναπές
soda i soda (fs)	σόδα
soft malakos	μαλακός
some merika	μερικά
some ligo (ms), ligi (fs), ligo (ns)	λίγο
something kati	κάτι
sometimes merikes fores	μερικές φορές
someone kapios	κάποιος
son o yios (ms)	γιος
song to tragudi (ns)	τραγούδι
sore epodinos	επώδυνος
soon sintoma	σύντομα
soup i supa (fs)	σούπα
sour ksini	ξινή
spaghetti spageti	σπαγγέτι
Spanish ispanika	ισπανικά
speak (v) milao	μιλάω
spoon to koutali (ns)	κουτάλι

spouse sizigos	σύζυγος
stairs, stairway skala	σκάλα
stamps ta gramatosima	γρααμματόσημα
station o stathmos (ms)	σταθμός
stay (v) meno	μένο
storm i kateyitha (fs)	καταιγίδα
story i istoria (fs)	ιστορία
straight evthia	ευθεία
street thromos	δρόμος
street othos	οδός
strong ishiros	ισχυρός
student mathitis	μαθητής
sugar zaHari	ζάχαρη
suitcase i valitsa (fs)	βαλίτσα
subway to metro (ns)	μετρό
summer to kalokeri (ns)	καλοκαίρι
sun o ilios (ms)	ήλιος
sunburn iliako ekavma	ηλιακό έγκαυμα
sunglasses ta yialia iliu (np)	γυαλιά ηλίου
sunblock anti-iliako	αντιηλιακό
supermarket super market	σούπερ μάρκετ
sweater zaketa	ζακέτα
sweet glikos	γλυκός
switch thiakoptis	διακόπτης
swim kolipi	κολύμπι
swim (v) kolibo	κολυμπώ

T

table to trapezi (ns)	τραπέζι
take (v) perno	παίρνω
taxi to taxi (ns)	ταξί
tea to tsai (ns)	τσάι
tea bag to fakelaki tsai (ns)	φακελάκι τσάι
teapot i tsagiera (fs)	τσαγιέρα
teacher o daskalos (ms)	δάσκαλος
teacher i daskala (fs)	δασκάλα
telephone tilefono	τηλέφωνο
television tileorasi	τηλεόραση
temperature i thermokrasia (fs)	θερμοκρασία
teller tamias trapezas	ταμίας τράπεζας
thanks efharisto	ευχαριστώ

then **tote**	τότε	
there **eki**	εκεί	
therefore **epomenos**	επομένως	
these, they av**ti**	αυτοί	
thing **pragma**	πράγμα	
think (v) **skeptome**	σκέπτομαι	
thirsty **thipsasmenos**	διψασμένος	
this av**to**	αυτό	
throat **lemos**	λαιμός	
ticket **to isitirio** (ns)	εισιτήριο	
time **ora**	ώρα	
timetable **hrono-thiagrama**	χρονοδιάγραμμα	
tire **lastiho**	λάστιχο	
today **simera**	σήμερα	
together **mazi**	μαζί	
toilet (ns) **i tualeta**	τυαλέτα	
tomato **domata**	ντομάτα	
tomorrow **avrio**	αύριο	
tonight **apopse**	απόψε	
too (more than required) **epipleon**	επιπλέον	
toothbrush **othondovurtsa**	οδοντόβουτσα	
toothpaste **othondopasta**	οδοντόπαστα	
tour **periothia**	περιοδεία	
tourist **touristas**	τουρίστας	
towel **i petseta** (fs)	πετσέτα	
tow truck **yeranos**	γερανός	
traffic light **fanari**	φανάρι	
train **to treno** (ns)	τρένο	
train station **stathmos trenon**	σταθμός τρένων	
travel (v) **taxithevo**	ταξίδεύω	
traveller **o taxithiotis** (ms)	ταξιδιώτις	
travel agency **taxithiotiko grafio**	ταξίδιωτικό γραφείο	
tree **to thendro** (ns)	δέντρο	
trip **to taxithi** (ns)	ταξίδι	
trousers **to panteloni** (ns)	παντελόνι	
truck **to fortigo** (ns)	φορτηγό	
truth **alithia**	αλήθεια	
turn! (vi) **stripste**	στρίψτε	
typical **tipikos**	τυπικός	

U

umbrella **i omprela** (fs)	ομπρέλα
uncle **o thios** (ms) **i thius** (mp)	θείος
under **ipo**	υπό
understand (v) **katalaveno**	καταλαβαίνω
unfortunately **thistohos**	διστολός
United States **inomenes polities**	Ηνωμένες Πολιτείες
until **mehri**	μέχρι
up **epano**	επάνω
urgent **epigon**	επείγων
usually **sinithos**	συνήθος

V

vacant, free **kenos**	κενός
vacation **thiakopes**	διακοπές
valley **i kilatha** (fs)	κοιλάδα
van **to fortigali** (ns)	φορτηγάλι
vegetable **to lahaniko** (ns)	λαχανικό
vegetarian **i hortofagos** (fs)	χορτοφάγος
vehicle **ohima**	όχημα
verb **rima**	ρήμα
very **poli**	πολύ
view **thea**	θέα
village **to horio** (ns)	χωριό
vinegar **to ksithi** (ns)	ξύδι
visa **i visa** (fs)	βίζα
visit **i episkepsi** (fs)	επίσκεψη
visit (v) **episkeptome**	επισκέπτομαι
voice mail **tilefoniti**	τηλεφωνητή

W

wait (v) **perimeno**	περιμένω
waiter **servitoros** (ms)	σερβιτόρος

waitress **servi<u>tora</u>** (fs)	σερβιτόρα
walk (v) **perpa<u>tao</u>**	περπατάω
want (v) **the<u>l</u>o**	θέλω
watch **ro<u>loi</u>**	ρολόι
water **to ne<u>ro</u>** (ns)	νερό
watermelon **kar<u>pou</u>zi**	καρπούζι
we **e<u>mis</u>**	εμείς
weak **at<u>hi</u>namos**	αδύναμος
weather **ke<u>ros</u>**	καιρός
week **i evtho<u>ma</u>tha** (fs)	εβδομάδα
weight **to varos** (ns)	βάρος
west **thi<u>si</u>**	δύση
wet **vre<u>me</u>nos**	βρεμένος
what? **ti?**	τι;
wheel **o tro<u>hos</u>** (ms)	τροχός
when? **po<u>te</u>?**	πότε;
where? **pu?**	πού;
which? **poios?**	ποιός
white **lef<u>ko</u>**	λευκό
who? **pios?**	ποιός;
why? **ya<u>ti</u>**	γιατί;
wife **i yi<u>ne</u>ka** (fs)	γυναίκα
window **to pa<u>ra</u>thiro** (ns)	παράθυρο
windshield **parm<u>priz</u>**	παρμπρίζ
windshield wipers **yalokatharis<u>ti</u>res**	υαλοκαθαριστήρες
wine **to kra<u>si</u>** (ns)	κρασί
winter **o hi<u>mo</u>nas** (ms)	χειμώνας
with **me**	με
without **ho<u>ris</u>**	χωρίς
woman **i yi<u>ne</u>ka** (fs)	γυναίκα
wonderful **i<u>pe</u>rohos**	υπέροχος
word **i <u>le</u>xi** (fs)	λέξη
work, job **i erga<u>si</u>a** (fs)	εργασία
work (v) **thu<u>le</u>vo**	δουλεύω
world **o <u>kos</u>mos** (ms)	κόσμος
write (v) **<u>gra</u>fo**	γράφω
writing **<u>gra</u>psimo**	γράψιμο

X

X-ray **actinogra<u>fi</u>a**	ακτινογραφία

Y

year o **hronos** (ms)	χρόνος
yellow **kitrinos**	κίτρινος
yes **ne**	ναι
yesterday **htes**	χτες
yet **akomi**	ακόμη
you **esis**	εσείς

Z

zero **mithen**	μηδέν

Greek - English Dictionary

All verbs are marked as (v).

A α alfa

actinografia ακτινογραφία	X-ray
achladi αχλάδι	pear
anglika Αγγλικά	English
aguri (ns) αγγούρι	cucumber
athelfi (fs) αδελφή	sister
athelfos (ms) αδελφός	brother
aera (ms) αέρα	air
aeroplano (ns) αεροπλάνο	airplane
erothromio (ns) αεροδρόμιο	airport
afino αφήνω	leave (v)
agapo αγαπώ	love (v)
ayelatha (fs) αγελάδα	cow
agorazo αγοράζω	buy (v)
agori (ns) αγόρι	boy
agora (fs) αγορά	market
agorazo αγοράζω	buy (v)
esthanonde αισθάνονται	feel (v)
ethousa αίθουσα	lobby
akomi ακόμη	yet
akriva ακριβά	expensive
akrivos ακριβός	exactly
akuo ακούω	hear (v)
akustika (np) ακουστικά	headphones
alati αλάτι	salt
alandika (fs) αλαντικά	delicatessen
alithia αλήθεια	truth
ala αλλά	but
amythala (np) αμύγδαλα	almonds
amesos αμέσος	immediately
an αν	if
ananas (ms) ανανάς	pineapple

a**na**pafsi ανάπαυση	rest
anatoli**ka** (fs) ανατολικά	east
anah**tiri** (ns) ανοιχτήρι	bottle opener
a**nex**othi ανέξοδη	inexpensive
an**th**ras (ms) άνδρας	man, husband
an**th**ropi (fs) άνθρωποι	people
anti-ilia**ko** αντιηλιακό	sunblock
apayo**revete** απαγορεύεται	forbidden
a**panthisi** (fs) απάνδισι	answer
apasholimenos απασχολημένος	busy
a**pen**anti απέναντι	opposite
ap**los** απλός	simple
a**po** από	from, door
a**po**yevma (ns) απόγευμα	afternoon
appose απόψε	tonight
aposke**ves** (fp) αποσκευές	baggage,luggage
apo**thehome** αποδέχομαι	accept (v)
aravi**kos** αραβικός	Arabic
ar**ga** αργά	late
argotera αργότερα	later
ariste**ra** αριστερά	left
a**risti** άριστη	excellent
arith**mo** αριθμώ	count (v)
arithmonihani (fs) αριθμονηχανη	calculator
arke**ta** αρκετά	enough
ar**ni** (ns) αρνί	lamb
artopo**lio** (ns) αρτοπωλείο	bakery
astinomi**kos** (ms) αστινομικός	police officer
astino**mia** (fs) αστινομία	police officer
astino**miko** **tmi**ma αστυνομικό τμήμα	police station
as**tra**galo (ms) αστράγαλο	ankle
a**ti**hima (ns) ατύχημα	accident
anelkis**tiras** (ns) ανελκυστήρας	elevator
a**thio** αντίο	goodbye
a**vrio** αύριο	tomorrow
av**to** (ns) αυτό	this
avti αυτή	she
avto**kin**ito (ns) αυτοκίνητο	car
av**tos** αυτός	he
av**go** αυγό	egg
av**ti** (ns) αυτί	ear
avtokini**to**thromo (ms) cαυτοκινιτόδρομο	highway

113

B β vita

banio μπάνιο	bathroom
vathis βαθύς	deep
valitsa (fs) βαλίτσα	suitcase
verikoko (ns) βερίκοκο	apricot
vivlio (ns) βιβλίο	book
vivlios (fs) βίβλιος	bible
vivliopolio (ns) βιβλιοπωλείο	bookstore
visa (fs) βίζα	visa
vlepo βλέπω	see (v)
vuno (ns) βουνό	mountain
voithisi βοηθήσει	help
vrathi (ns) βράδυ	evening
vrathino (ns) βραδινό	dinner
vrisko βρίσκω	find (v)
vrohi (fs) βροχή	rain
vromikos βρώμικος	dirty
vutiro (ns) βούτυρο	butter

Γ γ gama

galika Γαλλικά	French
ganthia (np) γάνδια	gloves
gala (ns) γάλα	milk
garaz (ns) γκαράζ	garage
gata (fs) γάτα	cat
yematos γεμάτος	full
yevma (ns) γεύμα	meal
yefira (fs) γέφιρα	bridge
yi (fs) γη	land
yaya (fs) γιαγιά	grandmother
yalia iliu (np) γυαλιά ηλίου	sunglasses
yatros (ms/fs) γιατρός	doctor
yati γιατί	because
nkremo (ms) γκρεμό	cliff
yios (ms) γιος	son
ya sas (plural, formal) γεια σας	hello, goodbye
ya su (singular) γεια σου	hello, goodbye

yenethlion γενεθλιον	birthday
yera<u>nos</u> γερανός	tow truck
yi<u>ne</u>ka (fs) γυναίκα	woman
gli<u>kos</u> γλυκός	sweet
<u>glom</u>bos γλόμπος	lightbulb
<u>glosa</u> (ns) γλώσσα	language
<u>gom</u>a (fs) γόμα	eraser
gonis (fs) γονείς	parents
go<u>nia</u> (fs) γονία	corner
<u>gra</u>fo γράφω	write (v)
<u>gra</u>psimo γράψιμο	writing
gram<u>mi</u> γραμμή	line
<u>gri</u>gora γρήγορα	quickly
gra<u>fio</u> (ns) γραφείο	office
grapefruit (ns) γκρέιπφρουτ	grapefruit
grama<u>tosi</u>ma (ns) γρααμματόσημα	stamps
gra<u>mi</u> (fs) γραμμή	line
<u>gri</u>gora γρήγορα	fast
yali<u>a</u> (np) γυαλιά	eyeglasses

Δ δ thelta

da<u>mas</u>kino (ns) δαμάσκηνο	plum
<u>das</u>kalos (ms) δάσκαλος	teacher
das<u>ka</u>la (fs) δασκάλα	teacher
<u>thah</u>tilo (ns) δάχτιλο	finger
<u>then</u>dro (ns) δέντρο	tree
despi<u>nis</u> δεσποινίς	Miss
thro<u>seros</u> δροσερός	cool
thexi<u>a</u> δεξιά	right
the<u>xi</u> δεξί	right (adj)
thi<u>ath</u>romo (ns) διάδρομο	aisle, row, corridor
thia<u>kopes</u> διακοπές	vacation
thia<u>kop</u>tis (ms) διακόπτης	switch
thia<u>mer</u>isma (ns) διαμέρισμα	apartment
thia<u>moni</u> (fs) διαμονή	accommodation
thiaforeti<u>kos</u> διαφορεικός	different
thia<u>vas</u>o διαβάσω	read (v)
thiava<u>ti</u>rio (ns) διαβατήριο	passport
thi<u>ef</u>thinsi (fs) διεύθυνση	address
thipsas<u>menos</u> διψασμένος	thirsty
ven<u>zi</u>ni (fs) δενζίνι	gasoline

115

doro (ns) δώρο	gift
thino δίνω	give (v)
thipla δίπλα	adjacent
thipsasmenos διψασμένος	thirsty
thiskolos δυσκολός	difficult
thiskolia δυσκολία	difficulty
thistohos διστολός	unfortunately
thorean δωρεάν	free of charge
thomatio (ns) δωμάτιο	room
thromos(ms) δρόμος	street

E ε epsilon

ego εγώ	I
ik εικ	fig
ime είμαι	to be (v)
isothos (fs) είσοδος	entrance
isitirio (ns) εισιτήριο	ticket
eki εκεί	there
eklisia (fs) εκκλησία	church
ekptosi έκπτωση	discount, sale
ektipotis (ms) εκτυπωτής	printer
elia (fs) ελιά	oil
eleolatho (ns) ελαιόλαδο	olive oil
elenika ελληνικά	Greek
endaxi εντάξει	ok
engoni (fs) εγγονή	grandchild/daughter
enesi (fs) ένεση	injection
engonos (ms) εγγονός	grandson
epano επάνω	up
epivatis (ms/fs) επιβάτης	passenger
epigon επείγων	urgent
epipleon επιπλέον	too (more than required)
episis επίσης	also
episkepsi (fs) επίσκεψη	visit
episkeptome επισκέπτομαι	visit (v)
episkipton (ms) επισκεπών	guest
epistoli (fs) επιστολή	letter (mail)
epithiho (fs) εποδοχή	reception
epikinthinos επικίνδυνος	dangerous
epihirison (fs) επιχειρήσεων	business

e**po**thinos επώδυνος	sore
epo**men**os επομένως	therefore
e**ri**mo (fs) έριμο	desert
eri**pi**a (np) ερείπια	ruins
e**ro**tisi (ns) ερώτηση	question
erhome έρχομαι	come (v)
e**sis** εσείς	you
estia**to**rio (ns) εστιατόριο	restaurant
eti**ma**zo ετοιμάζω	prepare (v)
e**ti**mos έτοιμος	ready
e**xo** έξω	outside
e**xo**thos (fs) έξοδος	exit
e**v**kolos εύκολος	early
efharisto ευχαριστώ	thanks
evtihis**men**os ευτυχισμένος	happy
efharistos ευχάριστος	pleasant
ev**thi**a ευθεία	straight
e**ho** έχω	have (v)
e**tho** εδώ	here

Ζ ζ **zi**ta

ze**no**nas (ms) ζενώνας	hostel
zevgos (ns) ζεύγος	pair, couple
zi**to** ζητώ	ask (v)
za**Ha**ri (ns) ζάχαρη	sugar
za**ke**ta ζακέτα	sweater
zo**i** (fs) ζωή	life

Η η **i**ta

ithi ήδη	already
ilia**ko** e**ka**vma ηλιακό έγκαυμα	sunburn
ino**men**es poli**ti**es Ηνωμένες Πολιτείες	United States
i**si**ha ήσυχα	quiet
ilios (ms) ήλιος	sun
ilia**ko** e**ka**vma ηλιακό έγκαυμα	sunburn

117

ilektrismos (fs) ηλεκτρισμός   electricity

Θ θ thita

thalasa (fs) θάλασσα	sea
thermasi (fs) θέρμασι	heating
thermokrasia (fs) θερμοκρασία	temperature
thia (fs) θεία	aunt
thios (ms) **thius** (mp) θείος	uncle
thea (fs) θέα	view

Ι ι yota

ispanika ισπανικά	Spanish
istoria (fs) ιστορία	story
ishiros ισχυρός	strong
isos ίσος	maybe, possibly

Κ κ kapa

ke και	and
kakos κακός	bad
katharos καθαρός	clean
kathe κάθε	every
kathome κάθομαι	sit (v)
kathreftis (ms) καθρέφτης	mirror
kalathi (ns) καλάθι	basket
kalamboki (ns) καλαμπόκι	corn
kalandika (np) καλλυντικά	cosmetics
kalos καλός	good
kalokeri (ns) καλοκαίρι	summer
kaltses (np) κάλτσες	socks
kamera (fs) κάμερα	camera

kamping κάμπινγκ	camping,campsite
kanapes (ms) καναπές	sofa
kanali (ms) κανάλι	canal
kano (ns) κανό	canoe
kano κάνω	do (v)
kapios κάποιος	someone
karavi (ns) καράβι	boat
kardia (fs) καρδιά	heart
karekla (fs) καρέκλα	chair
karoto (ns) καρότο	carrot
kart postal καρτ ποστάλ	postcard
karveli καρβέλι	loaf
kafsimon (ns) καυσίμον	fuel, gasoline
kashkol (ns) κασκόλ	scarf
kastro (ns) κάστρο	castle
kafe καφέ	brown
katalaveno καταλαβαίνω	understand (v)
katefunsi (fs) κατεύφυνση	direction
kateyitha (fs) καταιγίδα	storm
kati κάτι	something
kataskinosis (ms) κατασκίνοσις	campground
katigoria (fs) καταγορία	class
kafes (ms) καφές	coffee
katsika (fs) κατσίκα	goat
kato κάτω	down
kefali (ns) κεφάλι	head
kake (ns) κέικ	cake
kentro (ns) κέντρο	center
kenos κενός	vacant, free
kialia (np) κιάλια	binoculars
kilatha (fs) κοιλάδα	valley
kipos (ms) κήπος	garden
kinthinos κίνδυνος	danger
kiniti tilefono (ns) κινιτή τηλέφωνο	cellphone
kiklos (ms) κύκλος	circle
kirios κύριος	Mr.
kiria κυρία	Mrs.
kitrinos κίτρινος	yellow
klimatismu (ms) κλιματισμού	air conditioning
klimatisko (ns) κλιματισκό	air conditioner
klino κλείνω	close (v)
klistos κλείστός	closed
kori (fs) κόρι	daughter
koritsi (ns) κορίτσι	girl
kosmos κόσμος	world
kotopulo (ns) κοτόπουλο	chicken

ku**ver**ta (fs) κουβέρτα	blanket
ku**ta**li (ns) κουτάλι	spoon
kratisi κράτηση	reservation
krio κρύο	cold
ksiristi**ki** miha**ni** ξυριστική μηχανή	shaver
kav**to** καυτό	hot
kre**mas**tra (fs) κρεμάστρα	hanger
kre**mi**thi (ns) κρεμμύδι	onion
krevati (ns) κρεβάτι	bed
ktirio (ns) κτιρίο	building
kokinos κόκκινος	red
ko**li**pi κολύμπι	swim
koli**bo** κολυμπώ	swim (v)
kubi**a** (np) κουμπιά	buttons

Λ λ lamtha

lahani**ko** (ns) λαχανικό	vegetable
lampa (fs) λάμπα	lamp
lam**va**no λαμβάνω	receive (v)
lathi (ns) λάδι	oil
lastiho λάστιχο	tire
lef**ta** (np) λεφτά	money
lem**o**ni (ns) λεμόνι	lemon
le**mos** (ns) λαιμός	throat
leo λέω	say (v)
leofo**rio** (ns) λεωφορείο	bus
leo**fo**ros (fs) λεωφόρος	avenue
lep**to** λεπτό	minute
lexi (fs) λέξη	word
limni (fs) λίμνη	lake
lul**u**di (ns) λουλούδι	flower
ligo λίγο	a little, some

Μ μ mi

ma**kris** μακρύς	long

mala**kos** μαλακός	soft
mani**tari** (ns) μανιτάρι	mushroom
ma**theno** μαθαίνω	learn (v)
mathi**tis** (ms) μαθητής	pupil (student)
mati (ns) μάτι	eye
mavro μαύρος	black
maxi**lari** (ns) μαξιλάρι	pillow
me**yethos** μέγεθος	size
me**galos** μεγάλος	big
me**lisa** (fs) μέλισσα	bee
meli**tzana** (fs) μελιτζάνα	eggplant
me**no** μένο	live, stay, reside (v)
me**nu** (ns) μενού	menu
me**ra** (fs) μέρα	day
meri**kes fores** μερικές φορές	sometimes
me**si** μέση	middle
mesi**mera** (ns) μεσημέρι	midday
mesimeri**ano** (ns) μεσημεριαό	lunch
me**tro** (ns) μετρό	subway
mik**ros** μικρός	small
mi**lao** μιλάω	speak (v)
mi**lo** (ns) μίλο	apple
mi**nas** (ms) μήνας	month
mi**sos** μισός	half
mi**then** μηδέν	zero
mo**lini** (ns) μολύβι	pencil
mo**no** μόνο	only
mi**tera** (fs) μητέρα	mother
motosi**kleta** (fs) μοτοσυκλέτα	motorcycle
me**hri** μέχρι	until
mu**sio** (ns) μουσείο	museum
mi**kos** (ns) μήκος	length
mi**on** μείον	less
bal**koni** (ns) μπαλκόνι	balcony
ba**la** (fs) μπάλα	ball
ba**nana** (fs) μπανάνα	banana
ba**niera** (fs) μπανιέρα	bathtub
ban**io** (ns) μπάνιο	restroom
bata**ria** (fs) μπαταρία	battery
bira (fs) μπύρα	beer
ble μπλε	blue
bis**koto** (ns) μπισκότο	cookie
brosta μπροστά	in front of
bu**kali** (ns) μπουκάλι	bottle

N ν ni

ne ναι	yes
nikiazo νοικιάζω	rent (v)
noris νορίς	early
nostima νόστιμα	delicious
nosokomio (ns) νοσοκομείο	hospital
domata ντομάτα	tomato
duz (ns) ντους	shower

Ξ ξ ksi

ksana ξανά	again
ksenodohio (ns) ξενοδοχείο	hotel
ksero ξέρω	know (v)
ksiros ξηρός	dry
ksithi (ns) ξύδι	vinegar
ksini ξινή	sour

Ο ο omikron

othigos (ms) οδηγός	guide
othontiatro (ms/fs) οδοντίατρο	dentist
othondovurtsa οδοντόβουτσα	toothbrush
othondopasta οδοντόπαστα	toothpaste
othos οδός	street
othivo οδηγω	drive (v)
othivu (ms) οδηγού	driver
ohima (fs) όχημα	vehicle
ola όλα	all, everything
omprela ομπρέλα	umbrella
oston (ns) οστών	bone
uranos (ms) ουρανός	sky
ikoyenia (fs) οικογένεια	family

122

Π π pi

pi-mi π.μ.	a.m.
pago<u>to</u> (ns) παγωτό	icecream
pan<u>du</u> παντού	everywhere
pa<u>te</u>ras (ms) πατέρας	father
pale<u>os</u> παλαιός	old
pal<u>to</u> (ns) παλτό	coat
pan<u>to</u>te πάντοτε	always
pap<u>us</u> (ms) παππούς	grandfather
pap<u>u</u>tsi (ns) παπούτσι	shoe
pa<u>ra</u>thigma (ns) παράδειγμα	example
para<u>ken</u>tisi (fs) παρακέντηση	puncture
paraka<u>lo</u> παρακαλώ	please
parala<u>vi</u> (fs) παραλαβή	receipt
paral<u>ia</u> (fs) παραλία	beach, coast
pa<u>ra</u>thiro (ns) παράθυρο	window
par<u>ko</u>metro παρκόμετρο	parking meter
parm<u>priz</u> (ns) παρμπρίζ	windshield
<u>per</u>no παίρνω	take (v)
perio<u>thi</u>a περιοδεία	tour
perio<u>thi</u><u>ko</u> (ns) περιοδικό	magazine
pe<u>thi</u> (ns) παιδί	child
pe<u>thia</u> (np) παιδιά	children
pezopo<u>ri</u>a πεζοπορία	hiking
pezo<u>thro</u>mia (ns) πεζοδρόμιο	sidewalk
peri<u>so</u>tero περισσότερο	more
pet<u>se</u>ta (fs) πετσέτα	towel
pina<u>ki</u>tha (fs) πινακίδα	sign
<u>pi</u>no πίνω	drink (v)
pi<u>ru</u>ni (ns) πιρούνι	fork
<u>pi</u>o πιο	more
<u>pi</u>os Ποιός;	who?
pi<u>a</u>to (ns) πιάτο	plate
pi<u>ye</u>no πηγαίνω	go (v)
pi<u>xi</u>da (fs) πυξίδα	compass
plat<u>for</u>ma (fs) πλατφόρμα	platform
plin<u>ti</u>rio (ns) πλυντήριο	laundry
pliro<u>fo</u>ries (fs) πληροφορίες	information
pli<u>ro</u>no πληρώνω	pay (v)
pl<u>io</u> (ns) πλοίο	ferry, ship
<u>po</u>thi (ns) πόδι	leg
po<u>thos</u>fero ποδόσφαιρο	soccer

po**la** πολλά	many
po**li** πολύ	very
poli (fs) πόλι	city
poli**tis** (ms) πωλητής	salesman
poli**tria** (fs) πωλήτρια	saleswoman
poios ποιός	which?
ponos (ms) πόνος	pain
porta (fs) πόρτα	door
porto**ka**li (ns) πορτοκάλι	orange
pos πός	how?
posos πόσος	how much?
pota**mos** (ms) ποταμός	river
po**thi**lato (ns) ποδίλατο	bicycle
pote πότε	why?
po**te** ποτέ	never
po**ti**ri (ns) ποτήρι	glass
pu πού	where?
pukamiso (ns) πουκάμισο	shirt
puli (ns) πουλί	bird
pragma (ns) πράγμα	thing
prasinos πράσινος	green
prepi πρερι	must (v)
pres**vi**a (fs) πρεσβεία	embassy
priza (fs) πρίζα	electric outlet
proi (ns) πρωί	morning
proi**no** (ns) προινό	breakfast
proxe**ni**o (ns) προξενείο	consulate
proseramo**ye**a (ms) προσαμογέα	adapter
pro**so**po (ns) πρόσοπο	face
proso**hi** προσοχή	caution
proti**ma**o προτιμάω	prefer (v)
provo**le**on (ms) προβολέον	headlight
provlina (ns) πρόβλιμα	problem
ptisi (fs) πτήση	flight

Ρ ρ ro

rima (ns) ρήμα	verb
rizi (ns) ρύζι	rice
roz ροζ	pink
ro**tha**kino (ns) ροδάκινο	peach

roloi (ns) ρολόι   clock

Σ σ ς sigma

savvato Σάββατο	Saturday
salata (fs) σαλάτα	salad
saltsa (fs) σάλτσα	sauce
saloni σαλόνι	living room
sampuan (ns) σαμπουάν	shampoo
sandalia (np) σανδάλια	sandals
sapuni (ns) σαπούνι	soap
skolio (ns) σχολείο	school
stelno στέλνω	send (v)
sfigmos (ms) σφυγμός	pulse
signomi συγγνώμη	excuse me
simandiko σημαντικό	important
simera σήμερα	far, today
snehizo συνεχίζω	continue (v)
sinefo (ns) σύννεφο	cloud
singaritiria συγχαρήταρια	congratulations
sinomilia συνομιλία	conversation
sinithos συνήθος	usually
sintayi (fs) συνταγή	prescription
sizigos σύζυγος	spouse
skala (fs) σκάλα	stairs, stairway
skeptome σκέπτομαι	think (v)
skilos (ms) σκύλος	dog
skortho (ns) σκόρδο	garlic
snak (ns) σνακ	snack
soda (fs) σόδα	soda
sokolata σοκολάτα	chocolate
sorts (np) σορτς	shorts
spirta (np) σπίρτα	matches
supa (fs) σούπα	soup
spageti σπαγγέτι	spaghetti
spania σπάνια	rarely
spileo (ns) σπίλαιο	cave
spiti (ns) σπίτι	home, house
spitikos σπιτικός	homemade
stasi leoforio (fs) στάσι λεωφορείο	bus stop
stathmos (ms) σταθμός	station
stathmos trenon σταθμός τρένων	train station

125

stathmefsi στάθμευση	parking
stafili (ns) σταφύλι	grape
stafitha (fs) σταφίδα	raisin
stavros (ms) σταυρός	cross (religious)
stelno στέλνω	send (v)
stilo (ns) στυλό	pen
stis στις	at
stripste στρίψτε	turn! (vi)
strongilos στρογγυλός	round
simbules (fs) συμβολές	advice
shethon σχεδόν	almost
super market σούπερ μάρκετ	supermarket
soma (ns) σώπα	body

T τ taf

tahithromio (ns) ταχυδρομείο	post office
tamias trapezas ταμίας τράπεζας	bank teller
taxi (ms) ταξί	taxi
taxithi (ns) ταξίδι	trip
taxithiotis (ms) ταξιδιώτις	traveller
taxithevo ταξίδεύω	travel (v)
taxithiotiko grafio ταξίδιωτικό γραφείο	travel agency
telos (ns) τέλος	end
tenia (fs) ταινία	movie
tetarto τέταρτο	quarter
tilefono (ns) τηλέφωνο	telephone
tilefoniti τηλεφωνητή	voice mail
tileorasi (fs) τηλεόραση	television
timi (fs) τιμή	price
tipikos τυπικός	typical
tiri (ns) τυρί	cheese
traghuthi (ns) τραγούδι	song
tragutho τραγουδώ	sing (v)
trapeza (fs) τράπεζα	bank
trapezi (ns) τραπέζι	table
treno (ns) τρένο	train
tropos (ns) τόπος	place
tsai (ns) τσάι	tea
tsagiera (fs) τσαγιέρα	teapot
tsanda (fs) τσάντα	handbag

126

tsepi τσέπη	pocket
to το	it
tora τώρα	now
tote τότε	then
tou**ris**tas τουρίστας	tourist
tu του	of
tua**le**ta (ns) τυαλέτα	toilet
tzaba τζάμπα	free of charge

Υ υ **ip**silon

i**po** υπό	under
ipolo**gisti** (ms) υπολογιστή	computer

Φ φ fi

fakelos (ms) φάκελος	envelope
fake**la**ki tsai (ns) φακελάκι τσάι	tea bag
fako (ms) φάκο	flashlight
fa**na**ri φανάρι	traffic light
farma**ki**o (ns) φαρμακείο	pharmacy
farmako (ns) φάρμακο	medication
fao φάω	eat (v)
feta (fs) φέτα	slice
filos (ms) φίλος	friend
fili (fs) φίλι	friend
forema (ns) φόρεμα	dress
forti**go** (ns) φορτηγό	truck
forti**ga**li (ns) φορτηγάλι	van
fo**ti**a (fs) φωτιά	fire
ftano φτάνω	arrive (v)
fti**ah**no φτιάχνω	make (v)
fti**no** φτηνό	cheap
furnos (ms) φούρνος	oven
fotogra**fia** (fs) φωτογραφία	photograph
frenon (ns) φρένον	brake
fusta (fs) φούστα	skirt

127

X χ chi

hamburker χάμπουργκερ	hamburger
harti (ns) χαρτί	paper
hartis (ms) χάρτης	map
hirotehnia (fp) χιροεχνία	crafts
hrimata (np) χρίπατα	money
heri (ns) χέρι	hand
herete χαίρετε	hello
hronos (ms) χρόνος	year
hrono-thiagramma χρονοδιάγραμμα	timetable
hrostao χρωστάω	owe (v)
htena (fs) χτένα	comb
htes χτες	yesterday
hora (fs) χώρα	country
horio (ns) χωριό	village
hortofagos (fs) χορτοφάγος	vegetarian

Ψ ψ psi

psari (ns) psaria (np) ψάρι	fish
psilo ψηλό	high
psiyio (ns) ψυγείο	refrigerator
psomi (ns) ψωμί	bread

Ω ω omega

ora (fs) ώρα	hour, time

Verb Tables

This section gives a representative set of verbs with complete conjugation. Each verb shows the present, past and future tenses, as well as its imperative (command) form. This is the list of verbs:

arrive, ask, be, be able, buy, call, come, drink, eat, find, give, go, hear, know, learn, like, please, say, see, speak, take, travel, understand, want, write.

Arrive - fthano φθάνω

Present tense

I arrive	fthano	Φτάνω
You arrive	fthanis	φτάνεις
He/she/it asks	fthani	φτάνει
We arrive	fthanume	φτάνουμε
You arrive	fthanete	φτάνετε
They arrive	fthanun	φτάνουν

Past tense

I arrived	eftasa	έφτασα
You arrived	eftases	έφτασες
He/she/it arrived	eftase	έφτασε
We arrived	ftasame	φτάσαμε
You arrived	ftasate	φτάσατε
They arrived	ftasan	έφτασαν

Future tense

I will arrive	tha ftaso	Θα φτάσω
You will arrive	tha ftasis	Θα φτάσεις
He/she/it will arrive	tha ftasi	Θα φτάσει
We will arrive	tha ftasume	Θα φτάσουμε

You will arrive	tha **ftasete**	Θα φτάσετε
They will arrive	tha **ftasun**	Θα φτάσουν

Imperative

Arrive! (s)	**ftase**	φτάσε
Arrive! (p)	**ftaste**	φτάστε

Ask (for something) - zito ζητώ

Present tense

I ask	zi**to**	ζητώ
You ask	zitas	ζητάς
He/she/it asks	zitai	ζητάει
We ask	zi**ta**me	ζητάμε
You ask	zi**ta**te	ζητάτε
They ask	zi**tan**	Ζητάν

Past tense

I asked	**zi**tisa	Ζήτησα
You asked	**zi**tises	ζήτησες
He/she/it asked	**zi**tise	ζήτησε
We asked	zi**ti**same	ζητήσαμε
You asked	zi**ti**sate	ζητήσατε
They asked	zi**ti**san	ζήτησαν

Future tense

I will ask	tha zi**ti**so	Θα ζητήσω
You will ask	tha zi**ti**sis	Θα ζητήσεις
He/she/it will ask	tha zi**ti**si	Θα ζητήσει
We will ask	tha zi**ti**sume	Θα ζητήσουμε
You will ask	tha zi**ti**sete	Θα ζητήσετε
They will ask	tha zi**ti**si	Θα ζητήσει

Imperative

Ask! (s)	**zi**tise	ζήτησε
Ask! (p)	zi**ti**ste	ζητήστε

Ask (a question) - rot<u>a</u>o ρωτάω

Present tense

I ask	rot<u>a</u>o	ρωτάω
You ask	rotis	ρωτείς
He/she/it asks	rot<u>ai</u>	ρωτάει
We ask	rotame	ρωτάμε
You ask	rot<u>ate</u>	ρωτάτε
They ask	rot<u>un</u>	ρωτούν

Past tense

I asked	<u>ro</u>tisa	ρώτησα
You asked	<u>ro</u>tises	ρώτησες
He/she/it asked	<u>ro</u>tise	ρώτησε
We asked	<u>ro</u>tisame	ρωτήσαμε
You asked	<u>ro</u>tisate	ρωτήσατε
They asked	<u>ro</u>tisan	ρώτησαν

Future tense

I will ask	tha rot<u>i</u>so	Θα ρωτήσω
You will ask	tha rot<u>i</u>sis	Θα ρωτήσεις
He/she/it will ask	tha rot<u>i</u>si	Θα ρωτήσει
We will ask	tha rot<u>i</u>sume	Θα ρωτήσουμε
You will ask	tha rot<u>i</u>sete	Θα ρωτήσετε
They will ask	tha rot<u>i</u>sun	Θα ρωτήσουν

Imperative

Ask! (s)	rot<u>i</u>se	ρώτησε
Ask! (p)	rot<u>i</u>ste	ρωτήστε

I am - <u>ime</u> είμαι

Present tense

131

I am	ime	είμαι
You are	ise	είσαι
He/she/it is	ine	είναι
We are	imaste	είμαστε
You are	iste/isaste	είστε
They are	ine	είναι

Past tense

I was	imun	ήμουν
You were	isun	ήσουν
He/she/it was	itan	ήταν
We were	imaste	ήμαστε
You were	isaste	ήσαστε
They were	itan	ήταν

Future tense

I will be	tha ime	Θα είμαι
You will be	tha ise	Θα είσαι
He/she/it will be	tha ine	Θα είναι
We will be	tha imaste	Θα είμαστε
You will be	tha iste	Θα είστε
They will be	tha ine	Θα είναι

I can, am able - boro μπορώ

Present tense

I can	boro	μπορώ
You can	boris	μπορείς
He/she/it can, is able	bori	μπορεί
We can	borume	μπορούμε
You can	borite	μπορείτε
They can	borun	μπορούν

Past tense

I could, was able	boresa	μπόρεσα
You could, were able	boreses	μπόρεσες
He/she/it could	borese	μπόρεσε
We could, were able	boresame	μπορέσαμε
You could, were able	boresate	μπορέσατε
They could, were able	boresan	μπόρεσαν

Future tense

I will be able	tha boreso	Θα μπορέσω
You will be able	tha boresis	Θα μπορέσεις
He/she/it will be able	tha boresi	Θα μπορέσει
We will be able	tha boresume	Θα μπορέσουμε
You will be able	tha boresete	Θα μπορέσετε
They will be able	tha boresun	Θα μπορέσουν

Imperative

Be able! (s)	borese	μπόρεσε
Be able! (p)	boreste	μπορέστε

Buy - agorazo αγοράζω

Present tense

I buy	agorazo	αγοράζω
You buy	agorazis	αγοράζεις
He/she/it buys	agorazi	αγοράζει
We buy	agorazume	αγοράζουμε
You buy	agorazete	αγοράζετε
They buy	agorazun	αγοράζουν

Past tense

I bought	agorasa	αγόρασα
You bought	agorases	αγόρασες
He/she/it bought	agorase	αγόρασε
We bought	agorasame	αγοράσαμε
You bought	agorasate	αγοράσατε

They bought	agorasan	αγόρασαν

Future tense

I will buy	tha agoraso	Θα αγοράσω
You will buy	tha agorasis	Θα αγοράσεις
He/she/it will buy	tha agorasi	Θα αγοράσει
We will buy	tha agorasume	Θα αγοράσουμε
You will buy	tha agorasete	Θα αγοράσετε
They will buy	tha agorasun	Θα αγοράσουν

Imperative

Buy! (s)	agorase	αγόρασε
Buy! (p)	agoraste	αγοράστε

Come - erhome έρχομαι

Present tense

I come	erhome	έρχομαι
You come	erhese	έρχεσαι
He/she/it comes	erhete	έρχεται
We come	erhomaste	ερχόμαστε
You come	erheste	έρχεστε
They come	erhonte	έρχονται

Past tense

I came	irtha	ήρθα
You came	irthes	ήρθες
He/she/it came	irthe	ήρθε
We came	irthame	ήρθαμε
You came	irthate	ήρθατε
They came	irthan	ήρθαν

Future tense

I will come	tha ertho	Θα έρθω
You will come	tha erthis	Θα έρθεις
He/she/it will come	tha erthi	Θα έρθει

We will come	tha erthume	Θα έρθουμε
You will come	tha erthete	Θα έρθετε
They will come	tha erthun	Θα έρθουν

Imperative

Come! (s)	ela	έλα
Come! (p)	elate	ελάτε

Do - kano κάνω

Present tense

I do	kano	κάνω
You do	kanis	κάνεις
He/she/it does	kani	κάνει
We do	kanume	κάνουμε
You do	kanete	κάνετε
They do	kanun	κάνουν

Past tense

I did	ekana	έκανα
You did	ekanes	έκανες
He/she/it did	ekane	έκανε
We did	kaname	κάναμε
You did	kanate	κάνατε
They did	ekanan	έκαναν

Future tense

I will do	tha kano	Θα κάνω
You will do	tha kanis	Θα κάνεις
He/she/it will do	tha kani	Θα κάνει
We will do	tha kanume	Θα κάνουμε
You will do	tha kanete	Θα κάνετε
They will do	tha kanun	Θα κάνουν

Imperative

Do! (s)	kane	κάνε

Do! (p)	kanete	κάνετε

Drink - pino πίνω

Present tense

I drink	pino	Πίνω
You drink	pinis	πίνεις
He/she/it drinks	pini	πίνει
We drink	pinume	πίνουμε
You drink	pinete	πίνετε
They drink	pinun	πίνουν

Past tense

I drank	ipia	ήπια
You drank	ipis	ήπιες
He/she/it drank	ipi	ήπιε
We drank	ipiame	ήπιαμε
You drank	ipiate	ήπιατε
They drank	ipian	ήπιαν

Future tense

I will drink	tha pio	Θα πιω
You will drink	tha piis	Θα πιεις
He/she/it will drink	tha pii	Θα πιει
We will drink	tha piume	Θα πιούμε
You will drink	tha piite	Θα πιείτε
They will drink	tha piun	Θα πιουν

Imperative

Drink! (s)	pi	πιε
Drink! (p)	piite	πιείτε

Eat - f̲a̲o φάω

Present tense

I eat	tr̲o̲o	τρώω
You eat	tros	τρως
He/she/it eats	tr̲o̲i	τρώει
We eat	tr̲o̲me	τρώμε
You eat	tr̲o̲te	τρώτε
They eat	tr̲o̲ne	τρώνε

Past tense

I ate	e̲f̲aga	έφαγα
You ate	e̲f̲ayes	έφαγες
He/she/it ate	e̲f̲raye	έφραγε
We ate	f̲a̲game	φάγαμε
You ate	f̲a̲gate	φάγατε
They ate	e̲f̲ragan	έφραγαν

Future tense

I will eat	tha f̲a̲o	Θα φάω
You will eat	tha fas	Θα φας
He/she/it will eat	tha f̲a̲i	Θα φάει
We will eat	tha f̲a̲me	Θα φάμε
You will eat	tha f̲a̲te	Θα φάτε
They will eat	tha f̲a̲ne	Θα φάνε

Imperative

Eat! (s)	f̲a̲e	φάε
Eat! (p)	f̲a̲te	φάτε

Find - vrisko βρίσκω

Present tense

I find	vrisko	βρίσκω
You find	vriskis	βρίσκεις
He/she/it finds	vriski	βρίσκει
We find	vriskume	βρίσκουμε
You find	vriskete	βρίσκετε
They find	vriskun	βρίσκουν

Past tense

I found	vrika	βρήκα
You found	vrikes	βρήκες
He/she/it found	vrike	βρήκε
We found	vrikame	βρήκαμε
You found	vrikate	βρήκατε
They found	vrikan	Βρήκαν

Future tense

I will find	tha vro	Θα βρω
You will find	tha vris	Θα βρεις
He/she/it will find	tha vri	Θα βρει
We will find	tha vrume	Θα βρούμε
You will find	tha vrite	Θα βρείτε
They will find	tha vrun	Θα βρουν

Imperative

Find! (s)	vres	Βρες
Find! (p)	vrite	Βρείτε

Give - thino δίνω

Present tense

I give	thino	δίνω
You give	thinis	δίνεις
He/she/it gives	thini	δίνει
We give	thinume	δίνουμε
You give	thinete	δίνετε
They give	thinun	δίνουν

Past tense

I gave	ethosa	έδωσα
You give	ethoses	έδωσες
He/she/it gave	ethose	έδωσε
We gave	thosame	δώσαμε
You gave	thosate	δώσατε
They gave	ethosan	έδωσαν

Future tense

I will give	tha thoso	Θα δώσω
You will give	tha thosis	Θα δώσεις
He/she/it will give	tha thosi	Θα δώσει
We will give	tha thosume	Θα δώσουμε
You will give	tha thosete	Θα δώσετε
They will give	tha thosun	Θα δώσουν

Imperative

Give! (s)	those	δώσε
Give! (p)	thoste	δώστε

Go - piyeno πηγαίνω

Present tense (either of two words may be used)

I go	pao / piyeno	πάω / πηγαίνω
You go	pas / piyenis	πας / πηγαίνεις
He/she/it goes	pai / piyeni	πάει / πηγαίνει
We go, let's go	pame / piyenume	πάμε πηγαίνουμε
You go	pate / piyenete	πάτε / πηγαίνετε
They go	pane / piyenun	πάνε / πηγαίνουν

Past tense

I went	piga	Πήγα
You went	piyes	Πήγες
He/she/it went	piye	Πήγε
We went	pigame	Πήγαμε
You went	pigate	Πήγατε
They went	pigan	Πήγαν

Future tense

I will go	tha pao	Θα πάω
You will go	tha pas	Θα πας
He/she/it will go	tha pai	Θα πάει
We will go	tha pame	Θα πάμε
You will go	tha pate	Θα πάτε
They will go	tha pane	Θα πάνε

Imperative

Go! (s)	pae	Πάε
Go! (p)	piyene	Πήγαινε

Have - eho έχω

Present tense

I have	eho	έχω
You have	ehis	έχεις
He/she/it has	ehi	έχει
We have	ehume	έχουμε
You have	ehete	έχετε
They have	ehun(e)	έχουν

Past tense

I had	iha	είχα
You had	ihes	είχες
He/she/it had	ihe	είχε
We had	ihame	είχαμε
You had	ihate	είχατε
They had	ihan	είχαν

Future tense

I will have	tha eho	Θα έχω
You will have	tha ehis	Θα έχεις
He/she/it will have	tha ehi	Θα έχει
We will have	tha ehume	Θα έχουμε
You will have	tha ehete	Θα έχετε
They will have	tha ehun	Θα έχουν

Imperative

Have! (s)	ehe	έχε
Have! (p)	ehun	έχουν

Hear, listen - akuo ακούω

Present tense

I hear	akuo	Ακούω

You hear	a<u>ku</u>s	ακούς
He/she/it hears	a<u>ku</u>i	ακούει
We hear	a<u>ku</u>me	ακούμε
You hear	a<u>ku</u>te	ακούτε
They hear	a<u>ku</u>n	ακούν

Past tense

I heard	a<u>ku</u>sa	άκουσα
You hear	a<u>ku</u>ses	άκουσες
He/she/it heard	a<u>ku</u>se	άκουσε
We heard	a<u>ku</u>same	ακούσαμε
You heard	a<u>ku</u>sate	ακούσατε
They heard	a<u>ku</u>san	άκουσαν

Future tense

I will hear	tha a<u>ku</u>o	Θα ακούω
You will hear	tha a<u>ku</u>sis	Θα ακούσεις
He/she/it will hear	tha a<u>ku</u>si	Θα ακούσει
We will hear	tha a<u>ku</u>sume	Θα ακούσουμε
You will hear	tha a<u>ku</u>sute	Θα ακούσουτε
They will hear	tha a<u>ku</u>sun	Θα ακούσουν

Imperative

Hear! (s)	a<u>ku</u>se	άκουσε
Hear! (p)	a<u>ku</u>ste	ακούστε

Know - <u>ksero</u> ξέρω

Present tense

I know	<u>kse</u>ro	ξέρω
You know	<u>kse</u>ris	ξέρεις
He/she/it know	<u>kse</u>ri	ξέρει
We know	<u>kse</u>rume	ξέρουμε
You know	<u>kse</u>rete	ξέρετε
They know	<u>kse</u>run	ξέρουν

Past tense

I knew	ixera	ήξερα
you knew	ixeres	ήξερες
He/she/it knew	ixere	ήξερε
we knew	kserame	ξέραμε
you knew	kserate	ξέρατε
they knew	ixeran	ήξεραν

Future tense

I will know	tha ksero	Θα ξέρω
you will know	tha kseris	Θα ξέρεις
He/she/it will know	tha ksero	Θα ξέρει
we will know	tha kserume	Θα ξέρουμε
you will know	tha kserete	Θα ξέρετε
they will know	tha kserun	Θα ξέρουν

Imperative

Know! (s)	ksere	ξέρε
Know! (p)	kserete	ξέρετε

Learn - matheno μαθαίνω

Present tense

I learn	matheno	μαθαίνω
You learn	mathenis	μαθαίνεις
He/she/it learns	matheni	μαθαίνει
We learn	mathenume	μαθαίνουμε
You learn	mathenete	μαθαίνετε
They learn	mathenun	μαθαίνουν

Past tense

I learned	ematha	έμαθα
You learned	emathes	έμαθες
He/she/it learned	emathe	έμαθε
We learned	mathame	μάθαμε
You learned	mathate	μάθατε
They learned	emathan	έμαθαν

Future tense

I will learn	tha matho	Θα μάθω
You will learn	tha mathis	Θα μάθεις
He/she/it will learn	tha mathi	Θα μάθει
We will learn	tha mathume	Θα μάθουμε
You will learn	tha mathete	Θα μάθετε
They will learn	tha mathun	Θα μάθουν

Imperative

Learn! (s)	mathe	μάθε
Learn! (p)	mathete	μάθετε

Live/stay - meno μένω

Present tense

I live	meno	μένω
You live	menis	μένεις
He/she/it lives	meni	μένει
We live	menume	μένουμε
You live	menete	μένετε
They live	menun	μένουν

Past tense

I lived	emina	έμεινα
You lived	emines	έμεινες
He/she/it lived	emine	έμεινε
We did lived	miname	μείναμε
You lived	minate	μείνατε
They lived	eminan	έμειναν

Future tense

I will live	tha mino	Θα μείνω
You will live	tha minis	Θα μείνεις
He/she/it will live	tha mini	Θα μείνει
We will live	tha minume	Θα μείνουμε

You will live	tha minete	Θα μείνετε
They will live	tha minun	Θα μείνουν

Imperative

Live! (s)	mine	μείνε
Live! (p)	minete	μείνετε

Please areso αρέσω

Present tense

I please	areso	αρέσω
You please	aresis	αρέσεις
He/she/it pleases	aresi	αρέσει
We please	aresume	αρέσουμε
You please	aresete	αρέσετε
They please	aresun	αρέσουν

Past tense

I pleased	aresa	άρεσα
You pleased	areses	άρεσες
He/she/it pleased	arese	άρεσε
We did pleased	aresame	αρέσαμε
You pleased	aresate	αρέσατε
They pleased	aresan	άρεσαν

Future tense

I will please	tha areso	Θα αρέσω
You will please	tha aresis	Θα αρέσεις
He/she/it will please	tha aresi	Θα αρέσει
We will please	tha aresume	Θα αρέσουμε
You will please	tha aresete	Θα αρέσετε
They will please	tha aresun	Θα αρέσουν

Imperative

| Please! (s) | arese | άρεσε |
| Please! (p) | areste | αρέστε |

Read - thiavasa διάβασα

Present tense

I read	thiavasa	διάβασα
You read	thiavasis	διαβάσεις
He/she/it reads	thiavasi	διαβάσει
We read	thiavasoume	διαβάσουμε
You read	thiavasete	διαβάσετε
They read	thiavasun	διαβάσουν

Past tense

I did read	thiavasa	διάβασα
You did read	thiavases	διάβασες
He/she/it did read	thiavase	διάβασε
We did read	thiavasame	διαβάσαμε
You did read	thiavasate	διαβάσατε
They did read	thiavasan	διάβασαν

Future tense

I will read	tha thiavasa	Θα διαβάσω
You will read	tha thiavasis	Θα διαβάσεις
He/she/it will read	tha thiavasi	Θα διαβάσει
We will read	tha thiavasume	Θα διαβάσουμε
You will read	tha thiavasete	Θα διαβάσετε
They will read	tha thiavasun	Θα διαβάσουν

Imperative

| Read! (s) | thiavase | διάβασε |
| Read! (p) | thiavaste | διαβάστε |

Say - leo λέω

Present tense

I say	leo	λέω
You say	les	λες
He/she/it says	lei	λέει
We say	leme	λέμε
You say	lete	λέτε
They say	lene	λένε

Past tense

I said	ipa	είπα
You said	ipes	είπες
He/she/it said	ipe	είπε
We said	ipame	είπαμε
You said	ipate	είπατε
They said	ipan	είπαν

Future tense

I will say	tha po	Θα πω
You will say	tha pis	Θα πεις
He/she/it will say	tha pi	Θα πει
We will say	tha pume	Θα πούμε
You will say	tha pite	Θα πείτε
They will say	tha pun	Θα πουν

Imperative

Say! Tell me! (s)	pes	πες
Say! Tell me! (p)	pite	πείτε

See - vlepo βλέπω

Present tense

I see	vlepo	βλέπω
You see	vlepis	βλέπεις
He/she/it sees	vlepi	βλέπει
We see	vlepume	βλέπουμε
You see	vlepete	βλέπετε
They see	vlepun	βλέπουν

Past tense

I did see	itha	είδα
You saw	ithis	είδες
He/she/it saw	ithe	είδε
We saw	ithame	είδαμε
You saw	ithate	είδατε
They saw	ithan	είδαν

Future tense

I will see	tha tho	Θα δω
You will see	tha this	Θα δεις
He/she/it will see	tha thi	Θα δει
We will see	tha thume	Θα δούμε
You will see	tha thite	Θα δείτε
They will see	tha thun	Θα δουν

Imperative

See! (s)	thes	Δες
See! (p)	thite	Δείτε

Sleep - ki<u>ma</u>me κοιμάμαι

Present tense

I sleep	ki<u>ma</u>me	κοιμάμαι
You sleep	ki<u>ma</u>se	κοιμάσαι
He/she/it sleeps	ki<u>ma</u>te	κοιμάται
We sleep	ki<u>mo</u>maste	κοιμόμαστε
You sleep	ki<u>ma</u>ste	κοιμάστε
They sleep	ki<u>mun</u>te	κοιμούνται

Past tense

I slept	kimi<u>thi</u>ka	κοιμήθηκα
you slept	kimi<u>thi</u>kes	κοιμήθηκες
He/she/it slept	kimi<u>thi</u>ke	κοιμήθηκε
we slept	kimi<u>thi</u>kame	κοιμηθήκαμε
you slept	kimi<u>thi</u>kate	κοιμηθήκατε
they slept	kimi<u>thi</u>kan	κοιμήθηκαν

Future tense

I will sleep	tha kimi<u>tho</u>	Θα κοιμηθώ
you will sleep	tha kimi<u>this</u>	Θα κοιμηθείς
He/she/it will sleep	tha kimi<u>thi</u>	Θα κοιμηθεί
we will sleep	tha kimi<u>thu</u>me	Θα κοιμηθούμε
you will sleep	tha kimi<u>thi</u>te	Θα κοιμηθείτε
they will sleep	tha kimi<u>thun</u>	Θα κοιμηθούν

Imperative

Sleep! (s)	kimi<u>su</u>	κοιμήσου
Sleep! (p)	kimi<u>thi</u>te	κοιμηθείτε

Speak - mi<u>lo</u> μιλώ

Present tense

I speak	mi**lo**	Μιλώ
You speak	mi**las**	μιλάς
He/she/it speaks	mi**lai**	μιλάει
We speak	mi**lame**	μιλάμε
You speak	mi**late**	μιλάτε
They speak	mi**lan**	μιλάν

Past tense

I spoke	mi**lisa**	μίλησε
you spoke	mi**lises**	μίλησες
He/she/it spoke	mi**lise**	μίλησε
we spoke	mi**lisame**	μιλήσαμε
you spoke	mi**lisate**	μιλήσατε
they spoke	mi**lisan**	μιλήσαν

Future tense

I will speak	tha mi**liso**	Θα μιλήσω
you will speak	tha mi**lisis**	Θα μιλήσεις
He/she/it will speak	tha mi**lisi**	Θα μιλήσει
we will speak	tha mi**lisume**	Θα μιλήσουμε
you will speak	tha mi**lisi**	Θα μιλήσει
they will speak	tha mi**lisi**	Θα μιλήσει

Imperative

| Speak! (s) | mi**lise** | μίλησε |
| Speak! (p) | mi**liste** | μιλήστε |

Take - perno παίρνω

Present tense

I take	**perno**	παίρνω
You take	**pernis**	παίρνεις
He/she/it takes	**perni**	παίρνει
We take	**pernume**	παίρνουμε

You take	pernete	παίρνετε
They take	pernun	παίρνουν

Past tense

I took	pira	πήρα
you took	pires	πήρες
He/she/it took	pire	πήρε
we took	pirame	πήραμε
you took	pirate	πήρατε
they took	piran	πήραν

Future tense

I will take	tha paro	Θα πάρω
you will take	tha paris	Θα πάρις
He/she/it will take	tha pari	Θα πάρι
we will take	tha parume	Θα πάρουμε
you will take	tha parete	Θα πάρετε
they will take	tha parun	Θα πάρουν

Imperative

Take! (s)	parte	Πάρτε
Take! (p)	parete	Πάρετε

Think - skeptome σκέπτομαι

Present tense

I think	skeptome	σκέπτομαι
You think	skeptese	σκέπτεσαι
He/she/it thinks	skeptete	σκέπτεται
We think	skeptomaste	σκεπτόμαστε
You think	skepteste	σκέπτεστε
They think	skeptonte	σκέπτονται

Past tense

I thought	skeptika	σκέφτηκα
You thought	skeptikes	σκέφτηκες

151

He/she/it thought	skeptike	σκέφτηκε
We thought	skeptikame	σκεφτήκαμε
You thought	skeptikate	σκεφτήκατε
They thought	skeptikan	σκέφτηκαν

Future tense

I will think	tha skefto	Θα σκεφτώ
You will think	tha skeftis	Θα σκεφτείς
He/she/it will think	tha skefti	Θα σκεφτεί
We will think	tha skeftume	Θα σκεφτούμε
You will think	tha skeftite	Θα σκεφτείτε
They will think	tha skeftun	Θα σκεφτούν

Imperative

Think! (s)	skepsu	σκέψου
Think! (p)	skepstite	σκεφτείτε

Travel - taxithio ταξιδεύω

Present tense

I travel	taxithevo	ταξιδεύω
You travel	taxithevis	ταξιδεύεις
He/she/it travels	taxithevi	ταξιδεύει
We travel	taxithevume	ταξιδεύουμε
You travel	taxithevete	ταξιδεύετε
They travel	taxithevun	ταξιδεύουν

Past tense

I traveled	taxithefa	ταξίδεψα
You traveled	taxithefes	ταξίδεψες
He/she/it traveled	taxithefe	ταξίδεψε
We traveled	taxithefame	ταξιδέψαμε
You traveled	taxithefate	ταξιδέψατε
They traveled	taxithefan	ταξίδεψαν

Future tense

I will travel	tha taxi<u>thi</u>so	Θα ταξιδεύσω
You will travel	tha taxi<u>thi</u>sis	Θα ταξιδεύσεις
He/she/it will travel	tha taxi<u>thi</u>si	Θα ταξιδεύσει
We will travel	tha taxi<u>thi</u>sume	Θα ταξιδεύσουμε
You will travel	tha taxi<u>thi</u>sete	Θα ταξιδεύσετε
They will travel	tha taxi<u>thi</u>sun	Θα ταξιδεύσουν

Imperative

Travel! (s)	ta<u>xi</u>thepse	Ταξίδεψε
Travel! (p)	taxi<u>thi</u>ste	Ταξιδεύστε

Understand - katal<u>a</u>veno
καταλαβαίνω

Present tense

I understand	katal<u>a</u>veno	καταλαβαίνω
You understand	katal<u>a</u>venis	καταλαβαίνεις
He/she/it understands	katal<u>a</u>veni	καταλαβαίνει
We understand	katal<u>a</u>venume	καταλαβαίνουμε
You understand	katal<u>a</u>venete	καταλαβαίνετε
They understand	katal<u>a</u>venun	καταλαβαίνουν

Past tense

I understood	kat<u>a</u>lava	κατάλαβα
You understood	kat<u>a</u>laves	κατάλαβες
He/she/it understood	kat<u>a</u>lave	κατάλαβε
We understood	kat<u>a</u>lavame	καταλάβαμε
You understood	kat<u>a</u>lavate	καταλάβατε
They unserstood	kat<u>a</u>lavan	κατάλαβαν

Future tense

I will understand	tha katal<u>a</u>vo	Θα καταλάβω
You will understand	tha katal<u>a</u>vis	Θα καταλάβεις
He/she/it will understand	tha katal<u>a</u>vi	Θα καταλάβει

We will understand	tha katalavume	Θα καταλάβουμε
You will understand	tha katalavete	Θα καταλάβετε
They will understand	tha katalavun	Θα καταλάβουν

Imperative

Understand! (s)	**katalave**	κατάλαβε
Understand! (p)	**katalavete**	καταλάβετε

Want - thelo Θέλω

Present tense

I want	thelo	θέλω
You want	thelis	θέλεις
He/she/it wants	theli	θέλει
We want	thelume	θέλουμε
You want	thelete	θέλετε
They want	thelun(e)	θέλουν

Past tense

I wanted	thelisa	θέλησα
You wanted	thelises	θέλησες
He/she/it wanted	thelise	θέλησε
We wanted	thelisame	θελήσαμε
You wanted	thelisate	θελήσατε
They wanted	thelisan	θέλησαν

Future tense

I will want	tha theliso	Θα θελήσω
You will want	tha thelisis	Θα θελήσεις
He/she/it will want	tha thelisi	Θα θελήσει
We will want	tha thelisume	θα θελήσουμε
You will want	tha thelisete	Θα θελήσετε
They will want	tha thelisun	Θα θελήσουν

Imperative

Want! (s)	thelise	Θέλησε

Want! (p)	the**liste**	Θελήστε

Work - thu**lev**o δουλεύω

Present tense

I work	thu**lev**o	δουλεύω
You work	thu**lev**is	δουλεύεις
He/she/it works	thu**lev**i	δουλεύει
We work	thu**lev**ume	δουλεύουμε
You work	thu**lev**ete	δουλεύετε
They work	thu**lev**un(e)	δουλεύουν

Past tense

I worked	thu**lep**sa	δούλεψα
You worked	thu**lep**sis	δούλεψες
He/she/it worked	thu**lep**se	δούλεψε
We worked	thu**lep**same	δουλέψαμε
You worked	thu**lep**sate	δουλέψατε
They worked	thu**lep**sane	δούλεψαν

Future tense

I will work	tha thu**lep**so	Θα δουλέψω
You will work	tha thu**lep**sis	Θα δουλέψεις
He/she/it will work	tha thu**lep**si	Θα δουλέψει
We will work	tha thu**lep**sume	Θα δουλέψουμε
You will work	tha thu**lep**sete	Θα δουλέψετε
They will work	tha thu**lep**sun	Θα δουλέψουν

Imperative

Work! (s)	thu**lep**se	δούλεψε
Work! (p)	thu**lep**sete	δουλέψετε

Write - grafo γράφω

Present tense

I write	grafo	Γράφω
You write	grafis	Γράφεις
He/she/it writes	grafi	Γράφει
We write	grafume	Γράφουμε
You write	grafete	Γράφετε
They write	grafun	Γράφουν

Past tense

I wrote	egrapsa	Έγραψα
You wrote	egrapsis	Έγραψεις
He/she/it wrote	egrapse	Έγραψε
We wrote	grapsame	Γράψαμε
You wrote	grapsate	Γράψατε
They wrote	egrapsan	Έγραψαν

Future tense

I will write	tha grapso	Θα γράψω
You will write	tha grapsis	Θα γράψεις
He/she/it will write	tha grapsi	Θα γράψει
We will write	tha grapsume	Θα γράψουμε
You will write	tha grapsete	Θα γράψετε
They will write	tha grapsun	Θα γράψουν

Imperative

Write! (s)	grapse	γράψε
Write! (p)	grapste	γράψτε

Further Reading

Books

You will find these books very helpful.

Adams, Douglas Q. 1987. *Essential Modern Greek Grammar*, Dover Publications

Garoufalia-Middle, Hara. 2011. *Build Your Greek Vocabulary*, McGraw-Hill

Matsukas, Aristarhos. 2010. *Complete Greek*, Hodder Education

Websites

Here is a list of great web-sites that will help you learn more about Greek.

http://cooljugator.com/gr/

http://moderngreekverbs.blogspot.com/

http://www.xanthi.ilsp.gr/filog/

http://www.kypros.org/LearnGreek/

Made in the USA
Columbia, SC
23 March 2019